To Make The People Smile Again

A Memoir of the Spanish Civil War

by George Wheeler

Foreword by Jack Jones

Edited by David Leach

Zymurgy Publishing

United Kingdom 2003

Printed and bound by Bookmarque Ltd., Croydon, U.K.

 A CIP catalogue record for this book is available from the British Library.

ISBN 1 903506 07 7

© Zymurgy Publishing, Newcastle upon Tyne, United Kingdom 2003

George Wheeler was born in London in 1914. A skilled wood-machinist from a Labour Party background, he volunteered to serve in the International Brigade in spring 1938, and travelled to Spain in a group led by Jack Jones. Captured in the last action of the British Battalion, he spent seven months in a Nationalist concentration camp. He served in the British army during the Second World War, before returning to London and a long and happy marriage. Now a widower, he lives in Surrey.

Jack Jones was born in Liverpool in 1913. A dockworker and member of the Labour Party, he was appointed Political Commissar of the Major Attlee Company in the British Battalion of the 15th International Brigade. He went on to lead Britain's biggest union, the TGWU, and in retirement became a campaigner for pensioners' rights. He lives in London and is still active in the union's retired members' association.

David Leach was born in London in 1958 and grew up in England and Australia. His interest in the Spanish Civil War began as a history student at the University of Melbourne. His documentary film about Britons in the International Brigade, *Voices from a Mountain*, goes to air on the History Channel in spring 2003. He is married and now divides his time between London and southern Catalonia.

We came to Sunny Spain

To make the people smile again

And to drive the fascist bastards

From the hill and from the plain

Oh the Ri, Oh the Ri

Oh the Rio, Rio, Rio, Ha, Ha, Ha!

From a British Battalion marching song

Acknowledgements

A number of people across three continents helped in different ways to prepare *To Make The People Smile Again* for publication. In Europe, Richard Baxell, Tricia Bey, Helen Crosby, John Dixon, Cheli Durán, Martin Green, Helen Hunter, Bob Lambourne, Albertina Marfil, Craig McLaughlan, Nick Ridley, Leigh Riley, Billy Seago, Gareth Taylor, David Tormo Benavent and Dolly West Shaer; in the United States and Canada, Chris Brooks, Mora Gregg and Ross Roxburgh; and in Australia, Burt Bosma, Vivien Markham and Jenny Tarr.

Many thanks to the veterans, relatives and enthusiasts who allowed us to use photographs from their private collections.

Particular credit must go to the researcher Jim Carmody who supplied much of the biographical material for the endnotes. His knowledge of the British and Irish volunteers in Spain is astounding.

Credit too should go the publisher at Zymurgy, Martin Ellis, for identifying the merit in George's narrative. It must be instinctive, for Martin's maternal grandfather was Wally Tapsell, an iconic figure in International Brigade circles, who was killed in the retreats of spring 1938.

It is also appropriate here to acknowledge the International Brigade Association and its successor, the International Brigade Memorial Trust. This is a new organisation open to veterans, family members, friends and indeed anyone interested in the history and legacy of the British Battalion of the 15th International Brigade. Its website has contact addresses, information on International Brigade events, bibliographies and links to related sites and can be found at *www.international-brigades.org.uk*.

Foreword

Here is a most readable account of one young man's experiences as a volunteer in the legendary International Brigades during the Spanish Civil War.

It was indeed a new world for a young working man who had never ventured out of Britain before. Leaving family and friends behind, and giving up his job in the process, he went to defend the elected government of Spain in its struggle against the Franco rebellion. He knew of the threat to liberty posed by the Blackshirts and was appalled by the news of the massive support being given to the rebellion by Hitler's regime in Germany and by Mussolini's military and naval forces.

In a statement at the time, Major Clement Attlee (leader of the Labour Party) wrote, "An enormous weight of munitions has been thrown into the scale on the side of General Franco; heavy guns, up to date tanks and above all a huge reinforcement of the most modern and powerful aeroplanes have been sent off to aid the fascists. The splendid fighting spirit of the Republicans was overwhelmed by the sheer weight of metal...the plain fact is the British government acquiesces in aggression while pretending to support non-intervention".

No experienced politician, a young man in his twenties, George was prepared to give his all, risking life and limb and whatever hardship might be involved, to support what he believed to be the just cause of the beleaguered Republic.

The very human way he writes of his experiences will bring home to readers something of the commitment and endeavours of the International Brigade volunteers. In his case not just of directly fighting against the enemy, but also in the detailed accounts of his capture and of his pretty awful experiences as a prisoner in the camps and jails of the Franco regime.

The reality of the inhuman approach of Franco's power and its fascist nature is demonstrated by George Wheeler's description of the thuggery and sadistic treatment meted out by the jailers. It is heartening to read of the enduring spirit and determination of George and many of his fellow prisoners during that horrendous period.

The book is indeed a testimony to the indomitable spirit of the volunteers. As I write, George remains a member of the International Brigade Association and the Memorial Trust we have established in the UK and Ireland to maintain the numerous memorials which have been erected to the memory of the volunteers who made the supreme sacrifice during the Spanish Civil War.

In my view the cause was truly worthy and this book will add to others in helping to keep green the story of the International Brigaders with whom, like George, I was also proud to serve.

The contribution of David Leach in ensuring the preparation, editing and publication of the book deserves special mention and warmest appreciation.

Jack Jones
Transport House
London, January 2003

Introduction

To Make The People Smile Again goes to print as the author enters his ninetieth year. For George Wheeler, whose flowing white beard and powerful bearing suggest an Old Testament prophet, the past sixty-five years have been something of a bonus. On a hot September day in 1938, following the last action of the British Battalion in the Spanish Civil War, the young ginger-bearded Londoner stood and watched with six fellow International Brigade prisoners as their grave was slowly dug before them in the stony red soil of southern Catalonia.

George, as you will read, was very lucky indeed. Two and a half thousand men and women from Britain and Ireland went to Spain to fight fascism. Most were wounded and more than five hundred were killed. The boy from Battersea emerged from the war physically and mentally intact, his only scar the result not of gunshot or shellfire but a large boil.

Of the two thousand volunteers who returned to the British Isles, just over thirty survive as we enter 2003. It has been my privilege, in the last five years, to meet a number of men from this dwindling but vibrant group.

In summer 2000, while researching the life of a fallen volunteer commemorated in a rural Dorset churchyard (I recommend a visit to Powerstock and the family memorial to John Rickman, followed by a pint in the village pub), I attended an International Brigade function at a riverside park in Fulham, west London.

Afterwards, as a convoy of black limousines whisked away the local New Labour M.P, the mayor, Fulham's neighbouring mayors and a Spanish embassy representative and his retinue, I found myself walking with an International Brigade veteran who had been left to make his own way home.

As we progressed at an old man's steady pace across Putney Bridge and along Putney High Street, weaving our way between affluent Saturday afternoon shoppers towards the train station, I listened to a remarkable story from the Spanish Civil War. This sparky octogenarian, whom I now knew as George Wheeler, had - as a twenty-four year old - traversed the Pyrenees at night. He had fought bloody battles in the debilitating heat of a Catalonian summer. He had been captured by the fascists, faced summary execution on more than one occasion and spent seven months in one of Franco's concentration camps.

Our journey together on that warm August afternoon ended, with geographical symmetry, at Clapham Junction, the south London station where George's route to Spain had started so many years previously. As we parted, George casually mentioned that he had written a book about his service with the International Brigade.

It is estimated that there are some fifteen thousand books and pamphlets about the Spanish Civil War. Aside from the many political and social histories of the conflict, there are at least twenty published autobiographical accounts by British men who fought in Spain on the side of the Republic. A number of the earlier, self-consciously literary works helped to create and perpetuate the myth that the British Battalion was composed largely of Oxbridge poets.

A skilled manual worker from an industrial city who had left school at fourteen and endured poverty and periods of unemployment, George Wheeler was, as it were, the typical British volunteer. As the biographical details of George's comrades in the endnotes indicate, the Battalion was substantially proletarian in character and ethos: labourers, miners, dockers, clerks, shop assistants and factory hands. George's Battalion Commander had been a boilerman in Manchester.

A high proportion were members of the Communist Party; many, like George and Jack Jones, came from Labour Party backgrounds, while others had no overt political af-filiation. One of the principal strengths of George's book, it seems to me, is that it gives eloquent voice to the ordinary young working-class person of the 1930s who, at a critical point in our history, stood up to confront fascism.

Through conversations with George, and by reading the original manuscript of *To Make The People Smile Again*, I was inspired in 2001 to write and produce a documentary film about British volunteers in Spain called *Voices from a Mountain*. Together with the young director Andrew Lee, I filmed George, Jack Jones and three other veterans: the Welshman Alun Williams, the Scotsman John Dunlop and the Londoner Sol Frankel.

The experience of meeting and interviewing at length these bright, funny, reflective old men confirmed my impression - formed over leisurely glasses of *vino tinto* with George - that there was indeed something rather special about the International Brigade. On the day George was captured, a classical musician from Stockport called

George Green was killed in action. A month earlier he had written to his mother from Barcelona:

Mother dear, we're not militarists, nor adventurers nor professional soldiers. But a few days ago on the hills the other side of the Ebro, I've seen a few unemployed lads from the Clyde, and frightened clerks from Willesden stand up (without fortified positions) against an artillery barrage that professional soldiers could not stand up to. And they did it because to hold the line here and now means that we can prevent this battle being fought again on Hampstead Heath or the hills of Derbyshire.

Central to the narrative of *To Make The People Smile Again* are 'the hills the other side of the Ebro'. After interviewing George, Alun, John, Sol and Jack in Britain we flew to Spain to film the locations that feature so prominently in our veterans' oral testimonies. A comprehensive traveller's guide to the Ebro Offensive has yet to be written, and for our week in Catalonia, George's manuscript served as handbook and gazetteer.

The stretch of the River Ebro crossed by the British, and the towns and villages described by George, can now be reached within three hours by motorway and fast road from Barcelona. There is scant evidence, courtesy of Franco's vandals, that foreign volunteers ever came to Republican Spain. But in the main square at Marçà, a village George mentions, there is a relic of the 15th International Brigade. On the lintel above a garage door it is possible to make out the sign, in faded red paint, of the *Intendencia* - the Brigade stores. It is a curiosity, and worth the slight detour from the main road through Falset, not least because a few doors along, the *Café de la Plaça* offers an excellent *menú del día*.

Thirty-five kilometres across the River Ebro, beyond the olive groves and vineyards where George was captured, there is a startling reminder of the Spanish Civil War. The village of Corbera, as George observes, was destroyed by Franco's bombers and field guns. Today the old, hill-top centre of the village is exactly as it was when George came foraging for food and drink - a muddle of roofless, shattered houses and shops, where old doors hang at bizarre angles and ancient agricultural implements rust in ruined storerooms.

To commemorate the sixtieth anniversary of the conflict, old Corbera was transformed, with the contribution of local artists and sculptors, into a Monument to Peace - *Monument a la Pau in Catalan*. An 'Alphabet of Liberty' or *L' Abercedari de la Llibertat*, an installation of giant capital letters built from wood, metal and ceramics, now guides the visitor through the rubble.

In 2000 an International Brigade memorial of five metallic pillars, representing the continents from which the volunteers flowed into Spain, was unveiled on a high ledge in the old village. For anyone contemplating a trip to the Ebro battlefields, this vantage point - with its views across the valley to the mountains of the Sierra Caballs - is a fitting place to start.

Lower down, in new Corbera, construction continues on a museum devoted to the Battle of the Ebro. It is an ambitious project, initiated with funding from the Catalan regional government, and is scheduled to open in 2004. It promises to be a museum of ideas and interpretation, and will have a significant International Brigade content. One day I hope to see on display George's battlefield letters: he would have had his family believe he spent his time eating peaches and sunbathing.

It was a few kilometres up the road from Corbera, at the time George was penning reassuring notes to his mother and father at home in Battersea, that the British Battalion began to take heavy casualties on the steep hill outside Gandesa known to them simply as '481' or the 'Pimple'. Gandesa has its own Battle of the Ebro museum. It is a dreary and dispiriting place, with an emphasis on guns and barbed wire and tin helmets. There are a few too many framed photographs of Nationalist generals than is good for the digestion.

Fortunately the museum is only a few hundred metres from the Gandesa wine co-operative, an ornate modernist shrine to the grape designed by a pupil of Gaudi's. A sophisticated operation by local standards, the co-op offers free tastings, and after a few plastic thimbles of the fifteen per cent *vi negre*, *vi blanc*, *vi rosat* and *vi ranci*, an acapella rendition of the *Internationale* in the echoey entrance hall of the museum will present itself as a sensible idea.

Staff at the museum can give directions to Hill 481. The Nationalist positions are approached from a rough track on the outskirts of Gandesa. On a ridge leading towards the 'Pimple', victorious Nationalists erected a triumphal monument to themselves. Graffiti, in succinct Catalan, indicates what they might now do with their obelisk. The land around the monument is used, in an eloquent comment on the Franco regime, as an unofficial rubbish tip.

From this relatively high position you can look across to the limestone crags of the Sierra Pandols. We came to these mountains during our week in Catalonia to film a different sort of monument. In spring 2000 a crumbling memorial to the 15th International Brigade was discovered in the undergrowth on a remote mountainside, where it had lain undetected and undisturbed for more than sixty years. It is a squat, makeshift pyramid of three modest cement blocks, hurriedly built by a British military engineer during the intense heat and brutal fighting of August 1938.

Crudely inscribed in the cement are the names of thirty Britons, Canadians and Americans who died in the Ebro fighting. A number of them were known to George Wheeler, Jack Jones, Alun Williams, John Dunlop and Sol Frankel. The fallen volunteers' stories and the veterans' recollections formed the basis of our documentary.

In *To Make The People Smile Again* George writes about two of the best-loved (and most socially unrepresentative) members of the Battalion. The aristocratic Old Etonian Lewis Clive and the gentle Cambridge intellectual David Guest were killed on Hill 481 and while they, like all the British dead in Spain, have no known grave, their names were preserved on the Sierra Pandols memorial.

When we interviewed George in London, I asked him to talk about Lewis Clive and David Guest. George, if he will forgive me the impertinence, is an archetypal Anglo-Saxon male, and is not prone to displays of public emotion. But as he began to recreate the events recorded in his memoir, it was evident that Spain was not simply an episode in a long and creative life.

George spent just one year in Spain. Soon after returning to London he married his childhood sweetheart, the beautiful, apolitical Winnie. For five years he wore the khaki of the British Army, serving in a world war the International Brigade volunteers had tried to prevent. After the war George returned to practise his trade as a wood machinist at a workshop in London, cycling twenty miles to his bench every day for more than thirty years. The inchoate socialism of his youth matured into a commitment to the original principles of the Labour Party and an active role in the workshop as a trade unionist and shop steward. In the last decade he nursed his beloved wife through the terminal fog of Alzheimer's.

The candour and emotion George brought to the camera, the clarity with which he recalled Lewis Clive and David Guest and the Battle of the Ebro, was a forceful demonstration that Spain was the defining experience of his life. As *To Make The People Smile Again* shows, in the intense atmosphere of the International Brigade, George found that abstract notions like comradeship, egalitarianism, solidarity and internationalism could have genuine meaning. For George, and I suspect many veterans, Spain has always been just over the horizon.

David Leach

djrleach@hotmail.com
Batea, February 2003

Dedicated to the memory of my inspiration
my darling Winnie

GW

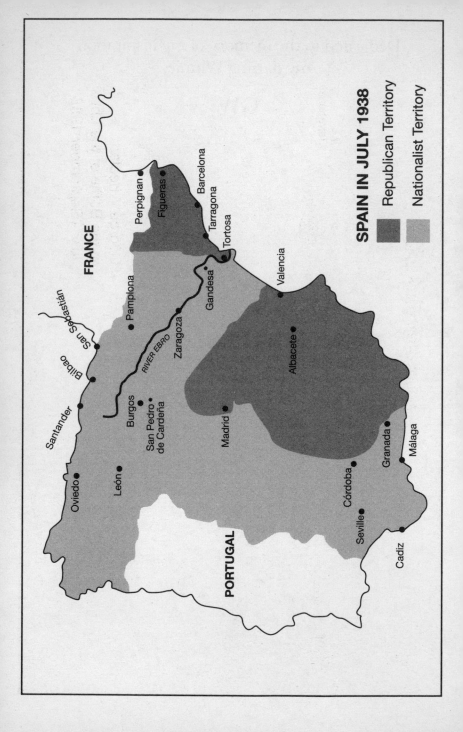

SPAIN IN JULY 1938

Republican Territory

Nationalist Territory

FRANCE

Perpignan

Figueras

Barcelona

Tarragona

Tortosa

San Sebastián

Pamplona

Gandesa

Valencia

Bilbao

RIVER EBRO

Zaragoza

Santander

Burgos

San Pedro
de Cardeña

Albacete

Oviedo

León

Madrid

Granada

Málaga

Córdoba

Seville

Cadiz

PORTUGAL

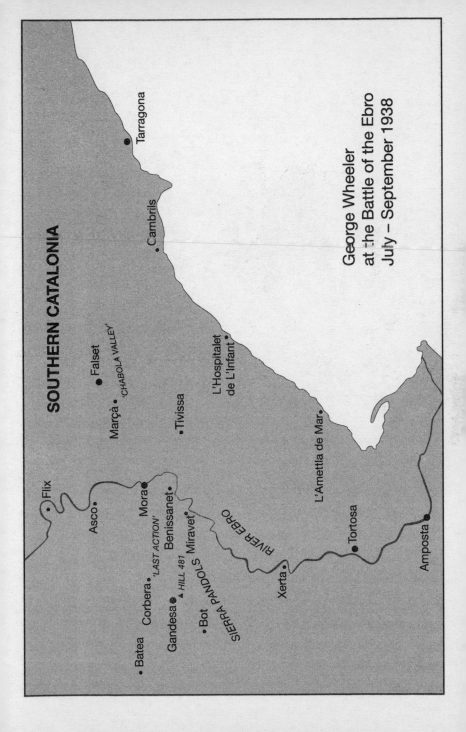

SOUTHERN CATALONIA

George Wheeler
at the Battle of the Ebro
July – September 1938

Tarragona

Cambrils

Falset
Marçà • 'CHABOLA VALLEY'

L'Hospitalet
de L'Infant

Tivissa

L'Ametlla de Mar

Flix
Asco •

Mora
Benissanet •

Batea
Corbera • 'LAST ACTION'
Gandesa • ▲ HILL 481
Miravet •
• Bot
SIERRA PANDOLS

RIVER EBRO

Xerta •

Tortosa •

Amposta •

Contents

1 The Black Hole

The squat, stone building lay in a field on the outskirts of the small, southern Catalonian town of Bot. Inside there was just one room, a work space where grapes were crushed for the local wine co-operative.

On a hot September night in 1938 it was not grapes that were crushed there, but men.

There were more than two hundred of us, including nineteen members of the International Brigade who had been captured earlier that day. We had already suffered many hazardous experiences: lined up by trigger-happy captors, kicked and cuffed and forced to march for hours in the sun, carrying our wounded with us. Not a drop of water had passed our lips.

As darkness came we were halted outside the building in the field. Tired and parched, we at least now had the prospect of a night's sleep. But then the doors were opened and we were herded into a 1930s version of the Black Hole of Calcutta[1].

When the doors were finally secured against us, there was just room to stand upright. The night seemed endless. Men slumped into an exhausted, sweating mass. The stench of body odour mingled with the sweet-sour smell of grapes. Sleep was impossible.

At dawn the doors were thrown open, and as weary bodies extracted themselves into standing positions, soldiers and *Guardia Civil*[2] appeared. They were armed with rifles and bayonets, which were used to drive us away from the doorway, where they then placed a table and two chairs.

It was a beautiful morning, and sunlight filtered through the leaves of a tree in front of the building, causing patterns to leap and dance on a stack of white paper that had been placed on the table by an orderly. A sergeant came forward with a paper in his hand.

"*¡Silencio!*" he roared, and as we fell quiet, he called out a name.

The previous day, after capture, we had been compelled to give our personal details. Now, the International Brigaders were summoned to the table in alphabetical order.

Each man was asked the same initial question.

"Why did you come to Spain?"

The answers given were more or less identical.

"Because I am an anti-fascist."

When the questioning of the first man was over, he was bundled out of the building and out of our sight. After a slight pause we heard a small burst from a light machine gun. The next man was called to the table and questioned in the same way. He too was taken outside and there followed a pause and another burst of fire. We appeared to be in trouble.

The process continued down through the alphabet. There was now no question in our minds, that after this perfunctory interrogation, we would be shot. Now, before each man was called, there were handshakes and farewells. There was no panic, no hysteria.

Because my surname starts with a 'W', I had some time to reflect on the events that had brought me to this old building near an obscure Catalonian town. And then finally it was my turn. After shaking hands with my three remaining comrades, I faced the interrogator.

"George Wheeler. Why did you come to Spain?"

Why did I go to Spain?

2 Battersea Volunteer

I was, of course, an anti-fascist. It was clear to me, as a young Londoner in the 1930s, that fascism was an attack on the working class; an attempt by the Right to suppress all opposition parties and trades unions. Their methods of crushing opponents, all too evident in Germany and Italy, were sickening in their brutality.

At the time I was living with my parents in Battersea, south London, and worked as a wood-machinist. My father was a socialist and I grew up in a relatively progressive political environment. I had read a little left-wing literature and attended the occasional political meeting or demonstration. But while my sympathies were always with the Left, I was never a member of the Communist Party.

I knew individual communists to be dedicated people who devoted their time to meetings, study groups and party work. I was too keen on football, swimming and boxing - a sport in which I had some moderate success locally - to worry about active politics.

Then, in the summer of 1936 came the rebellion in Spain. Unwilling to submit to the verdict of a General Election, the fascists - in collaboration with Hitler and Mussolini - rose against the government. With most of the regular army on their side, it looked as if the fascists would win easily. The people of Spain thought otherwise and fought back.

The valour and heroism of the Spanish people captured the admiration of the world. Had they been able to buy the arms to which, by international law, they were entitled, the fascists would have been smashed.

But Britain, France and the countries whose governments desired a fascist victory, perpetrated the scandalous sham of 'non-intervention'[3] which meant that while the fascists were receiving every kind of war material from Germany and Italy, the government side was getting very, very little. The Soviet Union and Mexico were the only countries to ignore this farcical arrangement, and sent what supplies they could.

The hypocrisy of non-intervention, which was so blatant, so transparent and so obvious, but against which we were so powerless, was perhaps one of the main factors that drew volunteers to the International Brigade.

On a spring afternoon in 1938, not long after my twenty-fourth birthday, I attended a rally in Trafalgar Square. The Labour politician Aneurin Bevan[4] gave an eloquent and impassioned address, denouncing the Tory government and non-intervention and urging support for the Spanish Republic. At that moment my mind was made up: I was going to Spain.

3 The Journey

I made tentative enquiries about the procedure for enlisting in the International Brigade. Contacts in the Communist Party directed me to an office in central London where I was interviewed and given a cursory medical examination. I was accepted.

Then came the awful task of telling my parents of my plans. How simple it is to decide on a course of action, providing it does not involve others. My father, I knew, would understand. He was a committed socialist with a long and proud record in the Battersea Labour Party. Active on our local 'Aid to Spain' committee, he could not reasonably dissuade me.

My mother, although supportive of him in every way, did not have my father's political insight or dedication. I now realise how she must have suffered when I told her of my decision. And how bravely she accepted it. In common with so many working-class mothers she had had her fair share of worry and trouble, particularly when unemployment was rife. Yet during these trying times her first consideration was always her children. As I explained my reasons for joining the fight in Spain, she purposely presented a calm exterior in order to make it easier for me.

The British government tried to dissuade young people from joining the fight in Spain by invoking an old law that made enlisting in a foreign army a criminal offence[5]. We had to act surreptitiously. I had been told to take very little luggage and to look like a weekend tourist[6]. On a bright

May evening, carrying a small case with a spare shirt, a change of underclothes and shaving kit, I travelled up to Victoria Station. There I first met Jack Jones[7], who had our tickets and instructions. We were joined by a tall, slim Australian called Kevin Rebecchi[8].

As our train to Newhaven was not due for an hour, we went to a pub where, over a meal of bread and cheese and beer, we introduced ourselves. Jack Jones, already prominent in the Labour Movement in Liverpool, told us about the political campaigns and anti-fascist activities in his home city. Of Kevin Rebecchi, we learned very little. A quiet fellow, he had worked his passage from Melbourne in order to be in the fight.

At Newhaven we boarded the boat for Dieppe. Our fellow passengers appeared to be genuine tourists, intent on enjoying a weekend break in Paris. It was my first trip abroad and I watched the preparations for departure with great interest, until at last the gangplanks were withdrawn and we were away.

It was a perfect night; millions of stars blinked in the night sky and the Channel was reassuringly still. The three of us leaned on the rail and watched the lights of England dwindling and disappearing in the distance. Conflicting emotions flooded through me as I stood there. Uppermost in my thoughts was my mother. How was she feeling now? Would I ever see her, my family and my native land again? My colleagues no doubt had similar feelings, and not a word was spoken until there was no longer any visible sign of England.

We docked at Dieppe in darkness and were soon on a train bound for Paris. Arriving at daybreak, we found the streets to be almost deserted. A café was open and we decided on a little refreshment before meeting our International Brigade contacts. I was surprised, at this early hour, to see Parisians chasing their coffee with shots of cognac. It was not something you saw dispensed with breakfast in Battersea. But as it was my first day in a foreign country it seemed appropriate to follow the local custom, and I ordered a glass.

After this pleasant early morning interlude, we left the café and went in search of an address in a working-class area of the city. We found it without difficulty and were immediately made welcome by our French comrades who took us to a co-operative café for breakfast. Over bowls of coffee and long loaves of French bread, we were introduced to the volunteers with whom we would be travelling down to Spain.

In addition to Jack and Kevin, our group now consisted of four Americans, a Mexican, another Australian called Jim McNeill[9] and a young Mancunian, Arthur Jamieson[10]. From a typical northern working-class background, he was pleasant and easygoing - the kind of boy who lived next door. I sat with two of the Americans, Jim Bayne[11] and Gus Mikadis[12]. They were warm and friendly men who made me laugh with the fast wit and complementary wisecracks of a double act.

With breakfast over, we were told our stay in Paris was to be short in duration. There was no time for sightseeing or exploration; we were to leave for the south of France that same day.

We were to book an early evening train to Nîmes, but were told to alight at Arles. This subterfuge was necessary owing to the sham of non-intervention. While Germany and Italy openly sent men and material into Spain, we were forced to cross the border illegally. A long, cross-country journey followed and, one by one, we dozed off. I awoke to daylight and the sight of unfamiliar scenery - a much drier land with vineyards and olive groves and stone-built, Roman-tiled farmhouses. For someone who had never been further south than Margate, these were indeed wondrous sights.

At Arles we split up into pairs and, following instructions, set off for the coach station. As Jim Bayne and I walked the streets of this ancient city, talking of our old lives in England and America, a firm friendship formed between us.

We took our seats on the coach and waited. Most of our friends were already seated, and gradually the coach began to fill with other men - all of them trying to look like tourists and all clearly on their way to fight in Spain. The coach left Arles southwards towards Perpignan. The road ran parallel to the coast and periodically I caught sight of a beautiful and very un-English blue sea.

We were indeed an unlikely bunch of holidaymakers on that coach driving south through a Mediterranean spring. It was not long before we were all trying to make contact with each other. And it was here I had my first encounter with the language barrier, for among us were many nationalities. I was among those who had no other language, and struggled to communicate. I watched with admiration as new European comrades switched with ease from French to German to English.

Night was falling as we reached our destination. The latter part of the ride had been along side lanes with dimmed lights, until finally we halted in the centre of a large field. Jumping down from the coach, we were led to a farmhouse. Dark and lonely it appeared as we approached, but light and lively as we entered. Long tables were laid as if for a feast. One of the organisers of the trip gave a short speech in French, which was then translated into English and German. It seemed we were to have a meal and then leave with the guides who would lead us across the Pyrenees and into Spain.

Others had arrived at the farmhouse before us, and there were more than fifty volunteers assembled for the meal. We enjoyed good country food and robust French table wines, with someone always on hand to refill our plates and glasses. This was my introduction to the personnel of the International Brigade and - in this atmosphere of warmth, good humour and genuine comradeship - I was greatly impressed.

I sat enveloped by the babble and chatter and looked intently around the tables. Here were men from all around the world who had left their homes to fight fascism. These, I thought, were the salt of the earth. How proud and exalted I felt to be one of them.

With the meal finally over, we were each given a pair of *alpargatas* - rope-soled sandals in common use in Spain and very useful for climbing mountains. Then began a long trek through back ways and along railway tracks, always keeping low to avoid detection by frontier guards. We were ordered to be totally silent, for the route was becoming increasingly difficult. At one point dogs barked furiously, and we feared we had been spotted. We froze and waited in the darkness until silence returned and we were able to proceed. At our next halt we were instructed to put on our *alpargatas*, and we realised we were at the foot of the mountains.

And so we began the long and hazardous climb over the Pyrenees; hazardous because in order to evade the non-intervention patrols, we were unable to use the regular paths. Indeed at times we formed a human chain to negotiate particularly rough passages.

But it was a marvellous night and, being young and fit, I really enjoyed the climb.

At frequent intervals a halt was called and we were able to enjoy a brief rest. During one of these stops we were provided with a real treat: a nightingale's song. It was as if he had waited until his audience had settled itself comfortably before beginning. Long before he reached his last glorious note we were spellbound. We waited patiently for an encore, but none came.

This was my first experience of mountainous terrain and I was surprised to see so much vegetation. Until now I had not associated trees with mountains, yet here high in the Pyrenees there were magnificently wooded slopes with firs and pines in abundance. The sharp scent of pine in the early morning air was wonderful.

Dawn was just breaking as we neared the summit, and a spectacular view opened up before us. Mountain mists swirled around high crags, forming strange and spectacular shapes, while rays from the rising sun bathed them in vivid colours. We were almost there.

Of the fifty who had started out, four were now in a state of near collapse and had to be carried. But we had reached the summit without losing anyone and, with light hearts and singing lustily, we began our descent into Spain.

Coming down was far easier and we made brisk progress. Approaching the foot of the mountains we passed many old Catalonian landworkers who raised their hands in the clenched fist salute and greeted us with *"¡Salud, camaradas!"* - Greetings, comrades! They were the first Spaniards we had ever seen and it was obvious by the warmth of their greeting that we were more than welcome in Government Spain.

The sun was now shining brightly and we could see clearly in the distance our next stop. It was a lonely mountain outpost manned by a squad of Spanish Republican soldiers. We arrived to an equally warm welcome and were informed by the officer in charge that transport had been arranged and would be coming shortly.

A cool mountain stream flowed by the outpost, and most of us peeled off our shirts and freshened ourselves with a brisk wash. After slaking our thirsts we sat or lazed in the sunshine in small groups, chatting, exchanging experiences, getting to know each other.

Sitting there, waiting for the trucks, I reflected on the last few days. I had progressed from being an onlooker to an active participant, prepared to do my best to defeat fascism and prevent another world war. I was now inside Spain and among men impelled by the same essential urge.

That it would be difficult we had no doubts. The military situation was extremely serious for the Spanish Republic, now split in two by a recent fascist offensive. Following many bloody battles, the Republicans had been forced back across the River Ebro, which now formed the front line in northern Spain.

Trucks arrived and we eagerly scrambled aboard. Bouncing around in the back, we sped along bumpy and dusty roads towards Figueras. Our view of the town was obscured by immense clouds of dust churned up by the vehicles. But as we neared the outskirts we turned off a main road and saw a big sign clearly displayed with an arrow pointing: *Las Brigadas Internacionales* - the International Brigades.

The trucks halted outside a large stone building with an iron staircase at each end. This was our barracks. Climbing a staircase, we entered the sleeping quarters - a large stone-floored hall containing three long rows of iron beds with a straw mattress on each.

After settling in, we were informed that a meal was ready. The mess room was in a separate building across the yard. We had just sat down to eat when whistles sounded and we heard a cry of "*¡avión!*" - aircraft! We were led hurriedly outside to a row of trenches, and there we waited until the planes had passed and the all-clear was sounded. No bombs were dropped. But this was excitement indeed: our first day in Spain and forced to take cover from fascist aircraft.

Back in the mess room we had our first Spanish meal of bread and a very tasty macaroni washed down with a sour red wine. We were told that the following day we would sign on as soldiers of the Spanish Republican Army.

Later, in the stillness of the Spanish night, I joined Jim Bayne and Gus Mikadis. We talked of our homes and our families. As I stood there, with my back against an olive tree and the Pyrenees in the near distance, I am not ashamed to say I felt just a little homesick.

4 The International Brigade

A bugle awoke us early the next morning. I hurried downstairs in order to avoid the queue at the water trough on a patio where we were to wash and shave and prepare for breakfast. Bread and coffee, served in the mess room, had rarely tasted so good.

Later that morning we were assembled in the yard and signed on as *soldados* - soldiers in the army of the Spanish Republic. Our pay was ten *pesetas* a day; approximately five pence at 1938 rates.

We were told that at the International Brigades' base we would undergo basic training in order to master our weapons, with plenty of marching and physical activity to prepare us for our respective national battalions.

Our chief mentor was a Spanish sergeant, a man possessed of infinite patience and good humour when dealing with the various nationalities under his command. It was explained that all commands were to be given in Spanish, so a list of the necessary orders was given to each man with instructions to learn and remember them. We formed ourselves into four squads in such a way as to avoid language difficulties.

In the days that followed, it became apparent that there was an appalling shortage of arms and equipment, and our training facilities were clearly inadequate. We understood we would have to learn soldiering the hard way, but to offset this we had a youthful enthusiasm and a dedication to the cause of the Republic.

In the evenings we had time for recreation. Chess, a game I had loved to play in Battersea, was popular among the volunteers. Football matches were played between all kinds of mixed teams, and what was lacking in skill was amply made up for in keenness and exuberance.

One evening, while a football match was in progress, we heard the *avión* warning whistles, and taking what cover we could, saw enemy aircraft approaching. Soon after they had passed over us, we felt the concussion and heard the explosions as Figueras was bombed. For most, this was our first experience of war and it had a sobering effect.

With the completion of our basic training, we were to move out to our respective national battalions. A batch of second hand and mis-matched uniforms had arrived at the base. Clad in odd combinations of shapeless and ill-fitting clothes, we now looked like extras in a Charlie Chaplin film. Each man had also been issued with a needle and thread, and over the next two or three days I was to witness impressive efforts in bespoke tailoring.

My own share of these cast-offs was a pair of trousers, shirt, jacket and a very tight pair of boots. I could either accept these or take a chance of acquiring a better fitting pair later on. My decision to put up with the immediate discomfort was, I think, a wise one. For though I suffered some inconvenience at first, they did gradually stretch and wear to my feet. The trousers and jacket fitted reasonably well, and with a little work with needle and thread I was fairly presentable.

At last we boarded trucks for the journey towards the front. Once again we bumped along on bone-jarring and dusty roads, but the scenery - which was severe and mountainous most of the way - was breathtaking in its beauty.

It was a long ride south, on a route that took us, without stopping, through Barcelona. We reached our destination, an International Brigade base in the central Catalonian town of Montblanc, late at night. In the morning we learned we were not yet with our battalions, and for a while would continue to train with the other nationals. This was good news for it meant we would remain with our American and other friends.

At Montblanc our training became more vigorous. The rough edges were being knocked off and we were becoming efficient soldiers. My own mental approach was undergoing a radical change. I was becoming more broadminded, more tolerant. I was roughing it, living in rough conditions with rough men and - strangely enough - enjoying it.

I was particularly drawn to my American buddies, Jim and Gus. We became almost inseparable. Gus was rather short of stature and very tubby. He had an infectious laugh and constantly wisecracked. Any hardship or difficulty was invariably turned into a joke. Jim was of medium height, lean and wiry, and had a dry sense of humour. Having worked for a time in Mexico, he knew a little Spanish and was able to help us with the language.

Training now concentrated on deployment and tactics for hill fighting. We were acting increasingly as a team - following, covering up and utilising each man's ability to the full. There was also more practice at the firing range, and we were becoming proficient in the use of the rifle and light machine gun.

Politically we were kept abreast of the latest news in Spain and the world situation in general through the medium of the Political Commissar[13]. Ours was an Austrian with an excellent record of anti-fascist struggle. Held prisoner by the Nazis, he had managed to escape and immediately joined the International Brigade, that being - as he said - the only logical course of action.

While we had a main assembly under the direction of the Austrian, we also managed our own English-speaking cultural and political hour. Jack Jones was elected political delegate and I was elected sports delegate. My duties were to organise football matches, boxing and athletic events and then submit reports for the wall newspaper.

Football remained the chief competitive sport at Montblanc, and I was kept busy arranging evening matches on the one available pitch. The games were popular occasions and always attracted large numbers of civilians who came to roar encouragement.

The political theory of anarchism had long roots in Catalonia, and it was perhaps inevitable that we would come into contact with some aspect of it. The unfettered self-government of the individual may be possible - and even probable - in the distant future, but when put into practice on a football field in 1938, it was chaotic.

A match had been arranged between two mixed sides of International Brigaders and all went well until half time. Our two teams moved off the field for a brief rest and then returned to take up their positions for the second half. As we did so, another two teams came on to the field and also took up their positions.

We protested that our game had not yet finished, expecting the newcomers to be reasonable and to wait until our game was over. But gesticulating wildly, they refused to move and even began playing. There were forty-four players on that field - some kicking the ball, others arguing, the rest looking completely nonplussed. After a while we gracefully retired, leaving the pitch to the anarchists.

On these warm June evenings a very popular place was a swimming pool among the rocks. It was a natural pool fed by a mountain stream. Water cascaded down the face of bare rock, across a wide table-like surface and then down into the pool. It was a deep pool, and here and there were rocks and ledges, splendid diving boards designed by nature. Jim, Gus and I made frequent visits. An hour or two here was always a refreshing end to a hard day's training and marching.

Some evenings the three of us went to a café in the town where we sat and drank wine and cognac and reminisced of schooldays, holidays, home life and girls. Gus was especially interested in girls, and when we heard what went on at another local café, he was very eager to pay it a visit. At first Jim and I tried to dissuade him, but we realised he was determined to go and reluctantly agreed to accompany him.

I had never before visited a brothel, so my reluctance to go with Gus must have been tempered with a certain degree of curiosity. That Jim and I would take no active part in proceedings was not due to superior moral virtues on our part. We were scared of disease. Being young and impressionable, I was even fearful of handling the glass containing the drink ordered by Gus immediately we arrived.

In fact the café was very similar in appearance to others we had visited in Montblanc, with a bar, tables and chairs and groups of customers talking and drinking. The only perceptible difference was the queue of men forming on a staircase that led to rooms above. Gus soon took his place in the queue.

Eventually he reappeared at the top of the stairs, an amused smile on his face and - completely unabashed - rejoined us at our table. Following this episode, I fully expected Gus to make further visits. But he was either entirely satisfied or totally disillusioned, for he never expressed the slightest desire to revisit the place.

The constant training was rapidly shaping us into good soldiers, and there was now a general desire to join our respective battalions in order to get to grips with the fascists. And when the move finally came, it came suddenly. I had no time to say goodbye to Jim and Gus. The order simply came to pack everything - and in a short while we were away on trucks towards the front. The war was coming closer.

5 The British Battalion

Our destination on this late June day was a range of hills between the towns of Falset and Marçà, where the British Battalion was regrouping after the spring retreats. The trucks halted in a camouflaged lay-by and we dismounted to be led to Battalion Headquarters.

We could see nothing from the road, but as we descended into a valley through a screen of trees and bushes, we came across a hidden wonderland of huts and lean-tos.

A particularly well-constructed hut served as Battalion HQ, where we were welcomed by the adjutant and allocated to different companies. Kevin Rebecchi - the Australian lad I had first met at Victoria Station - was placed with me in No. 4 Company. We teamed up with Harold Horne[14], a seasoned International Brigader who had recently returned from hospital.

Together we inspected our company lines and selected a site for our lean-to which we would build the following day. It was a good, secluded spot with a stone terrace wall against which we could erect our shelter. Putting our few belongings by the wall, we laid our blankets on beds of pine needles and slept with the stars above our heads.

The discipline was much more rigid here, as we discovered when a bugle woke us early the next morning. We heard the voice of our section leader Frank Proctor[15] exhorting us to get up:

"Come on lads, jump to it. You're in the army now!"

My limited experience as a soldier had already taught me one important lesson. If you wanted to keep clean, you had to get to the wash tubs early. And this I did on my first morning in Chabola Valley[16]. I was disconcerted to find that the only washing water available was in three small buckets. By the time my turn came the water was almost black with a thick layer of scum. Shortage of water was to be a constant theme during my time in Spain.

At our first Battalion parade that morning we learned that the newcomers would be excused duty for the day in order to build their *chabolas*. After breakfast I reported to Company HQ for tools with which to build and fashion our shelter. Collectively armed with one small, blunt axe, Harold, Kevin and I set out for the hills to cut wood.

Insufficiently equipped as we were, it was hard work under a hot sun. But by taking turns and with perseverance we felled two fir trees, which we dragged back to the valley. Trimming off the smaller branches, we used the trunks as supports, leaning them against the terrace wall, while the lower ends were sunk into the earth. We laced the smaller branches across the main supports, and soon had the basis of a good, sound structure.

Inside there was ample room for the three of us and our belongings. That night I lay on a bed of pine needles and looked up at the stars that shone through the gaps in our roof. It wasn't Battersea, but I felt very much at home.

At Montblanc we were practically all raw recruits with no experience of war. But here in Chabola Valley, Kevin and I were the new chaps training alongside the old campaigners. I soon settled down with my new comrades and found them to be a terrific bunch of men.

Harold Horne had taken part in many battles and had rejoined the battalion after recovering from wounds sustained in his last action. He was from Willesden, a fellow Londoner, and from listening to his recent experiences I was able mentally to prepare myself for the realities of war.

I made enquiries about another comrade from Battersea, Bert Sines[17], who was with a different company. When I found him and introduced myself, he was delighted to know I was the son of George Wheeler, whom he knew and respected for his work in the Labour Movement.

Bert had been in Spain for quite a while and wanted to know all the news from home. Reflecting on the political scene in Battersea, he called to mind the many meetings held in the Town Hall and on Clapham Common, at which my father figured prominently as a speaker.

He introduced me to the distinguished, gifted scientist and mathematician David Guest[18], who had recently joined the Battalion. David had sat on the Council in Battersea and also knew my father. His understanding of the political situation was evident to me, and on this - our first meeting - I felt I was in the company of an intellectual giant. Neither overbearing nor dogmatic, he was charming in manner.

Further down the valley were the lines of the Abraham Lincoln Battalion[19], and one evening I decided to visit their camp in the hope of seeing my American friends, Jim and Gus.

I set off on a track that ran along the valley floor. A mile or so into my hike I was hailed by a shout from the slopes above. Looking up, I was surprised to see the tubby figure of Gus accompanied by Jim. They had decided to try and contact me and luckily we had met half way. I took them back to the British lines.

They were impressed by the workmanship that had gone into the *chabola* and I began to feel houseproud - about a shack in a remote Catalonian valley. I introduced them to Harold Horne who had befriended an American, Harry Shepard[20], while in hospital. Jim and Gus promised to bring Harry with them on their next visit.

And so a social pattern developed in the valley. Jim, Gus and the affable Harry would visit our *chabola* with coffee or chocolate and occasionally a canteen of wine. Some evenings - armed with fruit and cigarettes - Harold, Kevin and I would hike down to the Abraham Lincoln camp, which was similar to ours in appearance with numerous huts cunningly concealed from aerial view.

These pleasant interludes - evenings spent with good friends in lively discussion and humorous debate in the warm night air - did not distract us from the principal reason behind this extended camping trip. We were soon to go into battle.

During the day we continued to train. I had my own rifle now, and considered it my most valuable possession. It was a *Mexicanski* rifle[21] with a long three-cornered bayonet that tapered down to a screwdriver point. I could strip and replace the bolt in rapid time and was developing a feel and affection for the weapon that only a soldier can know.

On the firing range I was a good shot, and added to my experience with practice on a Russian light machine gun. We all had practice and became proficient with hand grenades and, day by day, were becoming useful soldiers.

We were also becoming typical soldiers in another, less positive sense. We were lousy. I had reasoned that if one obeyed certain rules of cleanliness, these loathsome creatures could be kept in check. But with little water and no chance of a bath it was impossible. It was an everyday sight to see men delousing their shirts and pants, and a sense of revulsion never left me.

With training and guard duty and food detail, time passed swiftly. I had not had time to think about England. The first letter from home arrived, which I avidly read and re-read. My mother's pages contained family news and the straight heart-to-heart talk of a mother to her son. My father's broader vision and cheerful philosophy gave me tremendous encouragement. I missed my family, but any sense of homesickness had passed after the first days in Figueras. I was happy and proud to be with the International Brigade in Spain.

6 The Tragic Fiesta

We were told that a fiesta and sports meeting was to be held on July 18th to commemorate the beginning of the war. A football match was arranged between a mixed team of International Brigaders and a Spanish team. Several boxing contests were also on the bill and I was due to meet an American middleweight.

The day arrived and we assembled early before marching to Marçà where we paraded on a large piece of open ground. Other battalions were there, including the Americans and the MacKenzie-Papineau Battalion - or 'Mac-Paps' - the Canadian contingent in Spain[22].

Brigade officers gave rousing speeches, and we were addressed by the British Battalion Commander Sam Wild[23] and Commissar Bob Cooney[24]. The Commanders of the Lincolns and Mac-Paps also spoke. We gathered by the tenor of their words that something was in the air.

The fiesta began with the football match, followed by a series of track events. I was impressed by the standard of these amateur footballers and athletes and was moved to reflect on the high calibre of the men who had come to Spain to defend the Republic.

As the sporting contests ended, grub wagons appeared and we re-formed into our battalions to eat. The food was good that day. For, in addition to our usual rations of beans and stew, we were given fruit and chocolate. Cigarettes were distributed and bottles of Spanish champagne shared out among the men.

Sated and relaxed, we settled down, many hundreds of us in the afternoon sun, to watch the main attraction of the fiesta: the machine gun competition.

This was conducted in heats in which two crews at a time competed. Each crew had to run with their gun to a given spot and assemble, load, fire at a target and then unload. All went well and the competition was played out with great enthusiasm.

When the winners were announced, men surged on to the field, crowding around the guns, all interest and curiosity. Someone pressed a trigger. There was a report, a groan and three men were wounded - one seriously. He was a young Spaniard and had been hit in the stomach. It was a pitiful sight as he lay there calling for his mother while first aid men cut away his clothing and tried to staunch the flow of blood. I sensed that life was slowly ebbing away from him, and indeed he died on the way to hospital.

Two cartridges had been left in the gun's lock and this tragic accident brought the fiesta to a premature end. This was the first time I had witnessed such a poignant scene and it registered something of a shock. We marched sorrowfully back to camp.

Two nights later, after retiring for the night, we were woken by bugles and whistles and ordered to fall in with full equipment in thirty minutes. Out on the road we marched and began to conjecture about our destination. The general impression was that we would soon be in the thick of it. On and on we marched. Hours passed and a halt was called. Sentries were posted and we slept in the open.

Come the dawn, and still wondering, we marched straight back to camp.

That we were about to mount an offensive was fairly obvious, and each man made a point of checking his equipment and personal belongings. I had supplemented my own meagre equipment with a kind of rucksack-like holder to carry my small case on my shoulders. This I made from a good strong shirt that I had worn to Spain. Tearing it into strips, I had sewn and re-sewn them into straps which I criss-crossed and then attached to the case.

The result was not something you would see on display in the luggage department at Arding & Hobbs[25], but it would enable me to carry my shaving gear and personal effects, while leaving my hands free for my rifle. With the case permanently packed and available, I was now able to get ready in rapid time.

There was not long to wait, for on a baking late July afternoon we attended a Battalion meeting and were informed that we would shortly be moving out. We were going to the Ebro and would be marching at night and resting under cover by day. This news provoked tremendous enthusiasm and excitement.

That evening we fell in on the road and said farewell to Chabola Valley. And not without some sadness, for it held many pleasant memories. Friendships and associations flourished there, but also for many of us they ended there. I had last seen Jim and Gus at the fiesta and had since been unable to contact them. I surmised that the Americans would be on a different sector at the front, and I hoped I might see them again.

All night we marched. Trucks and artillery took the centre of the road with troops on either side. The element of surprise was to be the main factor in our offensive and the vehicles showed no lights. Fortunately there was some illumination from the moon and we were able to proceed at a good pace. Just before dawn we reached a heavily wooded area where we were to rest. Men and vehicles were well hidden here and, after posting sentries, we had a good sleep.

At dusk we resumed our march. The occasional whine of a shell reminded us that we were approaching the River Ebro and the frontline. A sudden explosion in our ranks made me dive instinctively to the side of the road. We feared an ambush, but in fact one of our company had dropped a hand grenade from his belt. It had been insecurely fixed and the pin came out. Luckily he was towards the tail of the column and only one man was slightly injured.

With the wounded man attended to, we continued on the road. The route took us through lush vegetation; we had entered a rich fruit-growing district very near the Ebro. Dawn was almost with us again when we halted in a dried up tributary of the main river.

With daylight came terrific heat, and I began to suffer the pangs of thirst. And while we had water in our water bottles, we had been encouraged to conserve as much as possible. There were potholes in the riverbed and many of them still contained water. It was dirty and stale and stagnant. But with the prospect of a whole day out in the sun, I took off my clothes and immersed myself in a pothole. Sitting there placidly with the dark, foul-smelling water up to my neck, I suddenly jerked upright. Heading towards me was a hideous creature, some five or six inches in length. It was the first scorpion I had ever seen. I recognised it from the picture books but was unaware that scorpions were indigenous to Spain. I would like to record that I staged a dignified, strategic withdrawal. Actually I jumped and ran.

Dressing myself, I rejoined the rest of the company which had found shade beneath a rocky outcrop. There, away from the glare of the sun, we waited. And then, as the sun began to drop behind a line of mountains to the west, the Battalion was called together.

We were addressed by Sam Wild and Bob Cooney, who outlined the plans for the next day. We were finally to cross the Ebro. The Spanish brigades were to have the honour of being the first to cross the river and would meet the first resistance. Our task was to exploit the position to the full and to push on as far as possible.

We were going into battle. This was inspiring news indeed and I felt simultaneously excited and apprehensive. We spent a marvellous, spirited evening and then, with clenched fists raised in salute, we sang the *Internationale* and retired to await the dawn.

7 We Cross The Ebro

Long before daybreak we were woken by the crack of rifle fire, the chattering of machine guns and the explosions of mortars and hand grenades. It was July 25th 1938 and the offensive had begun. Spanish troops, under Colonel Juan Modesto[26], had earlier rowed one hundred yards across the swiftly flowing river and advanced into fascist territory.

The surprise was complete and what resistance was offered was rapidly crushed.

To stem the advance Franco had immediately flung his planes into action. As we filed down into our positions behind tall reeds that lined the riverbank, we knew we would face incessant bombing.

The *avión* whistle blew and we concealed ourselves among the reeds. It was here that I had my first real experience of aerial bombardment. Looking up I could see the planes, big Italian bombers. I counted six of them gleaming in the early morning sunlight, and as I watched I could see bombs hurtling earthwards. They appeared to be coming straight towards me and, on hearing an awful screaming, swishing sound, I hugged the ground, which shook as I imagined an earthquake would.

Once, twice, three times they flew back. Each time was a nightmare as they dropped their hellish cargo. But worse was to follow as they flew lower and opened up with machine guns. I heard bullets cutting through the reeds above us and crashing into the earth just a few yards away.

After circling for a while, the planes flew off and we were able to proceed to the boats. Coming through a gap in the reeds we gained our first good view of the river and saw the damage already done by Mussolini's airforce. All along the banks were bomb craters while large pieces of wreckage floated downstream.

Seemingly unperturbed, engineers were feverishly busy, building pontoon bridges and cable ferries with flat-bottomed boats for heavy loads. Many of the men were in bathing trunks, assembling parts in the water in the face of constant attack from the air.

Taking our places in the boats we were rowed across, keeping a wary eye skywards, and as soon as we reached the opposite bank we leaped ashore. Working to practice, we waited long enough only to assemble in our sections and platoons, and then set off on the road at a smart pace.

The procedure during these visits was always the same. When the *avión* signal was given we immediately spread out in the fields on either side of the road and lay face downwards, making sure that anything shiny was concealed from the air. Though the planes attacked in waves, bombing and strafing anything that moved, little material damage was done. But they did slow us down and were a great strain on the nerves.

Racing on through the morning, we were now becoming accustomed to the sights and sounds of war. At a crossroads we came across groups of horses shackled and shot. The forward troops had captured many prisoners whom we saw being escorted back in batches, large numbers of Moors[27] among them. They appeared somewhat dazed, but were no doubt relieved to know that for them, at least, the war was over.

For us it was a matter of pushing on with all speed, the NCOs yelling and swearing, exhorting us to keep in contact with the unit in front and breaking us into a run when that contact was lost.

Someone in the ranks ahead of me began to sing. Soon we were all singing, the words rolling out across the valley to the rhythm of our marching feet. It was a song I had learned while training in Chabola Valley, and now it had a special resonance: "Oh we came to sunny Spain to make the people smile again. And to drive the fascist bastards from the hill and from the plain…"

With the sun blazing down on us from a cloudless sky the heat was almost overpowering, and our bulky packs were becoming heavy and cumbersome. By late afternoon we halted on the outskirts of the small town of Corbera. Progress was held up by a strong enemy group holding a strategic position in hills to our left, which covered the road and prevented the 13th Brigade[28] from entering the town.

Immediately in front of us was a small bridge over a dried-up river. We filed down to the riverbank, our movements concealed from the fascists by foliage and undulations in the ground. We were to use the riverbed as cover while we worked our way to the rear of their strongpoint. There was a gap in the protective screen of trees and bushes and as our men dashed across, enemy machine guns opened up. As I sprinted across this first piece of 'live ground' I lost my personal belongings. My homemade rucksack had let me down; the straps had worked apart and the case had fallen. But life had suddenly become too hectic for me to attempt to retrieve it.

We now had to work our way upwards and, putting our earlier training into effect, we began to move in formation, running from cover to cover, gradually getting nearer to the enemy in order to engage him. It was here that we suffered our first casualties.

Moving up, I took ccver behind a dead body. He was a Moor, and as I crouched there with bullets spitting around me, I became strangely fascinated with his feet. There were no boots or shoes on them and I noticed how immaculately the socks had been fitted over his pantaloons.

Progress was rather slow and protracted. It was late evening before we really got to grips with the fascists and dawn was breaking before we finally winkled them out. It had been a fierce and bloody encounter, and now - tired but victorious - we retraced our steps down to the road.

On the way back I found my case, but it had been cut open with a knife and all the contents taken. No doubt the finder thought the owner was one of the casualties: for him the spoils of war, for me just bad luck.

With the removal of the threat to their flank, the 13th Brigade entered Corbera and we moved on. The fighting was now practically all on hilltop positions, and without the support of artillery, aircraft and tanks, the task of taking a well-fortified hill was an extremely difficult one. Hill 481, nicknamed the 'Pimple', dominated the country for miles around and was considered the key to the strategic town of

Gandesa. Knowing this, the fascists had spared no effort in its defence.

As we took up our positions preparatory to going over for our first assault on the hill, we could not imagine the hardships and frustrations that lay in store for us. No. 1 Company was away on a mopping-up expedition, so Companies 2 and 4 were detailed for the first attack[29].

We were formed up into our squads, platoons and sections on a ridge facing the hill about one thousand metres from the enemy and waited for the order to attack. At last it came: "Over you go, lads!"

And bending almost double, we plunged over the crest. As each man went over he was, for a brief moment, a perfect target on the skyline before hurtling down the hill with bullets whistling all around.

It was hard going down a steep and wooded slope, and I soon went sprawling and lost my rifle. The air was dense with bullets that whizzed and ricocheted off rocks and trees. Hastily retrieving my rifle I safely reached the bottom of the hill where we were to assemble before pressing on. After a brief rest we began the climb up to the fascist positions until we were one hundred metres from them.

From here onwards there was practically no cover and it was obvious that a final assault would have been suicidal. We opened up a steady rifle fire, which they answered with a terrific bombardment, and it was all we could do to retreat to safer positions and hang on.

Thus the first attack on Hill 481 ended in failure. As it was impossible to get back to our positions in daylight we were compelled to wait until nightfall before returning. We had suffered many casualties. Harold Horne was one of these and was sent back to hospital. His place was taken by Sergeant John Dunlop[30], a tall Scotsman whom we knew to be an amiable and good-natured chap.

At dawn the next morning we made our second attempt on the hill and met with the same results. The offensive so brilliantly planned and executed by Colonel Modesto and the Spanish troops under Lister[31] was brought to a halt in our sector at Hill 481.

In the spring our forces had been thrown back across the River Ebro as a major fascist offensive drove a wedge through the Republic to the Mediterranean. The right-wing press in Britain was jubilant and prophesied the imminent fall of Barcelona. Valencia was threatened and indeed the end seemed near for democracy in Spain.

Then three months later the world suddenly gasped. Despite the constant attention of the Italian airforce, our army advanced on a one hundred and fifty kilometre front to a depth of thirty kilometres. Over five thousand prisoners were taken together with large quantities of military equipment. The fascists were well and truly on the run. Had non-intervention been a reality rather than a criminal one-sided sham, Franco would have been smashed and Hitler and Mussolini given a major rebuff.

8 Corbera

From the very beginning of the Ebro offensive, the bridges constructed by our engineers were repeatedly damaged by fascist bombers, causing considerable delays in the supply and distribution of munitions and food.

In the four days since we crossed the river we had received no food and had to rely on iron rations. I had lost mine when my case had fallen and was now distinctly hungry.

Meanwhile, Corbera was now unoccupied. It was decided that we should send in a patrol to forage for food and drink, and I immediately volunteered, motivated as much by a rumbling stomach as a sense of duty.

Carrying extra water bottles, four of us set off, descending from our secure ridge position into the valley. It was too dangerous to take the main road, which was under constant shellfire. Once again we took cover in a dried-up riverbed and, hidden from enemy observers, soon reached the outskirts of the town.

Here we decided to split in pairs and began a systematic search for anything edible. It was evident that all the shops and storehouses had been thoroughly combed by other patrols, so we devoted our attentions to a house-to-house search. There was plenty of wine in the cellars, and after sampling a little we filled our bottles. But of food there was no sign.

Entering one house through a smashed wall, we searched a larder. On a shelf was a large jug of jam, with a layer of mildew about an inch thick. Finding a spoon we scraped off the mildew and ate the jam. It was delicious.

Moving on, we came across a shop. The frontage was blown in and the first floor hung precariously. Impelled by hunger we went in and gingerly climbed a broken-down staircase to search among the wreckage. To our immense delight we found a sack of biscuits. A further search revealed a small bunch of dried raisins.

We decided to appease our hunger there and then. Sitting in the dust and rubble, I enjoyed the finest meal I have ever eaten: a hard biscuit and a few raisins, washed down by a swig of wine. As we ate we heard the approach of enemy aircraft and, looking up through the shattered roof, saw three planes circling the town. They dropped several bombs and promptly flew away.

Continuing our search we found nothing more than a few nuts, which we pocketed and then set off to meet our two colleagues. Making our way through what had clearly been Corbera's main thoroughfare, we were appalled at the havoc and destruction. There were several dead mules and horses in the street and the stench was nauseating. I pictured in my mind how this delightful little town must have looked before the fascist bombs and shells had reduced it to ruins.

Returning safely to our lines, we handed over our meagre booty to the Quartermaster for equitable distribution among the men. Hunger soon returned.

The attacks on Hill 481 continued. Each day we ran, crawled and stumbled towards the top. Assaults were mounted from different directions but ended with identical results. How we prayed for planes and tanks to assist us against this fortress.

Food kitchens had finally got through, and with our first good meal in days came a ration of cigarettes. A non-smoker, I put them in my pocket and forgot about them.

During one attack on the hill, a number of us regrouped under cover before continuing our climb to the fascist positions. Most of the men were inveterate smokers and had long since finished their ration.

One exclaimed, "What I'd do for a smoke right now!" The others concurred.

"Will these do?" I said, and tossed the packet to them. To my comrades, at that moment, I was an angel from the skies.

After a smoke they all felt better and we continued our ascent. This time our hope was to get close enough to hurl hand grenades into the concrete pillbox on the crest of the hill. Once again the advantages were overwhelmingly greater for the defender than the attacker.

Sorrowfully we retreated, and even more sorrowfully we counted our dead and wounded. Our losses were steadily increasing, the strength of our companies gradually dwindling. Familiar, cheerful and friendly faces were missing every day. Some, thankfully, were only wounded and sent back across the river to hospital. But others had paid the full price, staining the thin soil of Spain with their life's blood.

9 Deaths On A Hill

Individual acts of bravery and courage became almost commonplace on the field of battle and I have witnessed many. Here I must record the magnificent fortitude of Lawrence Pryme[32] of London.

He was of frail build, a rather quiet man, but with the heart of a lion. In any action Lawrence always distinguished himself and, by his coolness under fire, inspired others to give of their best.

One night in early August we were again attacking Hill 481. It was a cloudy night and the darkness gave us plenty of cover, enabling us to approach the top of the hill. Crawling on our bellies we were making good progress when the moon, in all its beauty, suddenly appeared from behind a cloudbank. From total darkness to silvery whiteness in seconds and our movement was seen. There was a burst of machine gun fire and Lawrence, who was a few yards in front of me, was hit.

I remained still and quiet and mercifully another cloud blanketed the moon. I crawled carefully towards Lawrence and asked him if he could crawl back with me. He couldn't move. Stretching out my arm I whispered, "Give me your hand, Lawrence." I began to pull him towards me.

We wore hard leather ammunition pouches on our waist belts and, as I pulled Lawrence across the rough ground, they made a scraping sound that carried across the night air. There was another burst of machine gun fire. Waiting until it was quiet, I crept nearer to him and unbuckled his belt and discarded his pouches. As I did so he quietly remonstrated with me to leave him. He had been shot through both legs, one bullet had smashed the bone at the thigh and he was bleeding badly. I dragged him a little further and another man joined me.

We agreed that it would be impossible to lift him, so I acted as human stretcher. Lying on my back we tenderly eased Lawrence on to me and I held him in my arms. I noticed how one leg seemed to have no connection to his body and it twisted around in a sickening manner. Both his legs were saturated in blood, and as I was dragged out of range of the fascist bullets, carrying Lawrence with me, so I was aware of the warm sticky gore that now permeated my own clothing.

Lawrence Pryme died. He had lost too much blood and while being dragged over that rough ground must have suffered untold agonies, for he was fully conscious all the time. Not once did he whimper or cry out. I am proud to have fought alongside him.

Our Company Commander had received injuries in a previous encounter and was now in hospital. Lieutenant Lewis Clive[33], himself just returned from hospital, took over.

We were now attacking Hill 481 from many different directions. On a night attack several of us got close enough to the summit to throw hand grenades. As usual our supplies were limited and the attack began to lose momentum. In the artificial light caused by fire and explosions I could see my comrade Taffy Brickell[34]. His eyes bulged with Welsh fury as he called in vain for more grenades and cursed the hypocrites who deprived us of the weapons we so sorely needed.

Lewis Clive excelled himself as Company Commander. He was everywhere: directing, organising, encouraging. One morning he selected three of us to take up vantage points on a ridge facing the fascists. We were instructed to keep up a constant rifle fire on their position.

I was in a rather exposed spot; my only cover a gorse bush. I concentrated my aim on a movement I detected at the base of an enemy pillbox and fired round after round until my rifle bolt became almost too hot to handle.

Lewis Clive re-appeared and asked about the activity in the fascist lines. It was a hot, sunny day and, as usual, my shirtsleeves were rolled up. At that moment I felt splashes on my forearm, and glancing down, was astonished to see they were splashes of blood. Turning, I saw Lewis reel and fall. Someone below said "What a ghastly sight."

I slid down from my firing position and saw that the top of his head was severed completely and, as he lay there, the brain was spilling from its case. It was indeed a ghastly sight.

The death of Lewis Clive was instantaneous. A former Oxford rowing blue and Labour Councillor for Kensington, he was said to be a descendant of Clive of India. This big, cheerful and sincere man had performed his duties as Company Commander with distinction. Well liked and respected in the battalion, this was a great loss to us all.

From the very start of the offensive, one of our chief worries was thirst, and our water bottles were invariably empty. The grapes in the vineyards were not yet ripe; we tried crushing them but the juice was unpleasant and made thirst more severe. Unripe tomatoes gave similar results.

There was a water hole some kilometres away and two of us were selected to find it and bring back some of this precious fluid. My colleague was an old campaigner who knew something of the hills and was confident of locating the waterhole.

We set off with as many water bottles as we could manage. Slung over our shoulders on long leather straps, they were awkward and cumbersome. Taking well-worn paths, we trudged on - now climbing, now descending. The sun blazed down on us from a cloudless sky, as it had done for weeks. My partner, whom I knew only as 'Snowy'[35], was full of confidence when we started out, so I left the pathfinding to him. Occasionally a stray shell would scream over - a grim reminder that we were still in the firing line.

I detected a worried frown on Snowy's face and he confided that he feared we had strayed into enemy territory. Loaded as we were with the canteens, and with the straps cutting into our necks and shoulders, the sweat literally poured off us. Neither of us had a watch and we lost all track of time. It seemed we had walked for hours and then, as we approached a slight rise, we sensed we were near water. There must have been humidity in the air.

A network of dry irrigation ditches led us to a patch of higher ground. And here we found a *pozo*, a type of well that had been in use for hundreds of years in Spain. As we neared the well, we broke into a run, the empty bottles clanking around us. We pulled eagerly on a wooden arm that propelled a line of buckets up from the well and over a stone trough. Cold, clean water cascaded into the trough, and we fell to our knees and drank deeply.

Our thirsts sated, we began systematically to fill the water bottles and lined them up ready for departure. Snowy was eager to leave, but the sight of so much water in the trough was irresistible. I was in a dirty, dusty state and my shirt and trousers were stiff with the dried blood of Lawrence Pryme. I decided to take a bath and rinse my clothes.

"George, it's too dangerous", protested Snowy. "We could be in enemy territory",

"Bugger enemy territory and bugger Franco", I said and stripped off.

As I sat splashing away in the trough, poor Snowy became increasingly agitated. And his fears were indeed justified. For hardly had I finished bathing when the fascists began shelling. They had obviously had the *pozo* under observation and in range of their artillery. The shells landed uncomfortably close and I was compelled to dress quickly. We hurriedly gathered up the canteens and, oppressed by the weight of the water, stumbled away from the shellfire.

Taking what we considered would be a short cut, we found ourselves a long way out and missed certain landmarks. We were clearly lost, and the heat, perspiration and the awkward loads we carried, combined to give us the jitters. And then anxiety gave way to relief and jubilation as we recognised a rocky outcrop beyond which our company waited.

We got back to our lines safely enough, but death and severe wounds continued to take a steady toll of our company's strength. Each day we either saw or heard of someone who had paid the full price. It was at this time that I heard with profound sorrow of the death of David Guest. A brilliant mathematician, scientist, author and philosopher, his death at the age of twenty-seven was a grievous loss to the working-class movement.

10 Respite From Battle

On a stifling August night we were relieved. In darkness the Battalion filed away from positions on Hill 481 and began the long descent to the road. On the way we passed the Spanish unit that was taking over from us. Cheerful and encouraging greetings passed between the two groups.

Once on the road we formed up into our companies and began to march. We stopped near a large vineyard and settled down to a night's sleep away from the bullets and shells and mortars.

On waking the next morning, the atmosphere was reminiscent of Chabola Valley. I enjoyed a hearty breakfast of fried bread and sardines washed down with coffee. What a relief it was to be away from the frontline.

At a Battalion meeting that morning, we were told we would enjoy a short respite and would re-organise to prepare for further action. Our losses, although severe, would be augmented by those returning from hospital. With a little re-shuffling we would be ready once again.

I was promoted to the rank of *Cabo* - Corporal, reporting to the amiable and able Sergeant John Dunlop. As we rested, the first consideration in the military sense was the overhauling of our weapons. All rifles and light machine guns were stripped, cleaned and oiled. And when these and other mundane but vital tasks were completed, we had time for relaxation.

John Dunlop and I found time to explore the district, and this we did at our leisure in the nature of Sunday afternoon strolls. One difference from an amble across Clapham Common or through Battersea Park, however, was that we always carried our water bottles, constantly alert for a water supply.

One afternoon we learned of the existence of a well just a few kilometres away from our camp. Following the route given us by our informant, we covered the estimated distance but found no sign of the well. Somewhat despondent we carried on when suddenly John let out a whoop of joy: there in front of us was the object of our search.

This was not a *pozo*, but simply a deep hole with a bucket on a rope, just like a conventional English well. Eagerly we lowered the bucket expecting to hear a pleasant splash as it hit the water. Instead there was a metallic clang as the bucket hit hard ground. The well was dry.

This possibility had not occurred to us. But John gave a rueful grin and suggested going back a different way. I readily agreed in the hope that we might yet find water, and we struck out across country. We plodded on, neither meeting anyone nor seeing human habitation, and all the while becoming thirstier.

Almost at the point of giving up, we saw some farm buildings and a small cottage, where we were sure we would find refreshment. We knocked on the door, which was opened by an elderly man, and John, who could speak some Catalan, asked if he could spare us some water.

He took us into a scullery and from a large earthenware jug poured us each a mug of cool water. We drank greedily.

The old man told us that there were only three of them there: himself, his wife and sister, who came and greeted us. They were elderly folk and we marvelled that they could carry on the farm work on their own.

Although water was scarce, they readily allowed us to quench our thirst and fill our canteens. They told us they were five or six kilometres from Benissanet, a small town in the fruit-growing land by the River Ebro. Being so close to the river, they had been constantly bombed since our offensive began, and the whole population had been evacuated. These three had nowhere else to go and were determined to stay.

John conversed with them for a long while, and I could tell that his charm of manner really impressed them. Wonderfully hospitable people, they invited us to call in any time. With night falling, we left for our company lines, where we discovered that others had already paid a visit to Benissanet. They confirmed the farmer's story of evacuation and desolation. Apparently there was plenty of fruit in the district and no one to tend it. John and I decided to go the next day.

After fulfilling our morning duties, we scrounged a couple of sacks and set off towards the river. The terrain was rugged and rocky in parts, and on one stretch of road the dust was inches thick. As each foot descended, so a cloud of dust arose and we were soon choking. Fortunately we had water and were able to slake our thirst. And then, as we neared the river, the ground became less rocky and more trees appeared. Gradually green and succulent vegetation came into view, and we were on the outskirts of Benissanet.

There was ample evidence of recent visits by Franco's planes, and we entered a deserted town. With no sign of life anywhere, we began to wonder if we were doing the right thing and began to feel a little guilty. But the knowledge that the fruit and other edibles would surely go rotten if left convinced us that this was not looting.

The first house we came to had the front door half blown off its hinges and was hanging precariously. Carefully pushing it aside, we went through and into the back garden where we beheld a wondrous sight: a garden laden with all kinds of produce. There were apples, greengages, potatoes, tomatoes, aubergines and onions. We wondered about the orderliness of it all. Then, to our astonishment, we saw two chickens in a crudely built hen coop. Surely, we thought, there must be someone here to tend them. To make sure, we began shouting and whistling.

The sudden noise in that deserted place startled the wild bird life into a loud chorus. But there was no other response to our shouts, and we were satisfied that we were the only people there. We decided to take the chickens, but there remained the task of killing them. John said that he couldn't possibly do it, so the job was left to me, and I had never killed a chicken before. I rehearsed with several imaginary twists and then swiftly seized the first one, and pulled and twisted its neck. I killed it. I didn't like what I was doing but immediately repeated the performance on the second chicken.

With all the death and destruction around us, how absurd it seemed that we should be affected by the killing of two chickens. My hands were trembling as we hurriedly thrust them into one of the sacks. I wanted to get them hidden from my sight as quickly as possible.

The potatoes then received our attention and we pulled a good supply. Then followed onions, apples and tomatoes. While we were under a tree picking greengages, three fascist planes appeared and circled the town. We froze and remained perfectly still while they flew back and forth. They dropped no bombs and eventually flew off.

Moving back into the house, we decided to have a good look around and, leaving our laden sacks by the doorway, ascended a set of badly damaged stairs. We entered a large room at the front of the house and, out of simple curiosity, began to examine pictures and photographs and ornaments. We had no intention of looting the house, and each item we replaced.

As we prepared to leave, we heard a commotion in an adjoining room. An old man emerged, struggling into his trousers and protesting vehemently. He was, not unnaturally, a little upset, and he berated us in Catalan. The only word I understood was *comandante,* which he used in every sentence, and inferred he was going to report us to our commander. It was some time before he calmed down sufficiently for John to explain that we were not going to rob him.

We each gave him one hundred *pesetas* to compensate for the produce we had taken and assured him we had acted of complete ignorance of anyone's presence in the town. John even managed to get him to see things from our point of view and before we left he shook hands with us. On the way back - and for a long while afterwards - we conjectured on why he stayed in the town and often wondered what happened to him.

We carried the sacks of food back to the farm and gave the major proportion of the fruit and vegetables and one of the chickens to the old folk. Then we asked if they would cook the other one for us and whether we could bring the six other members of my squad the next day to share a good meal. They were, of course, delighted with the foodstuffs we had given them and readily agreed to our request.

And what a meal we enjoyed in that lonely, isolated farmhouse. The chicken was stewed with vegetables and a little garlic. Local wines, both red and white, were brought to the table. Fresh fruit, nuts and raisins were produced for a second course. Our comrades declared it to be the best meal they had had in months.

John and I made frequent visits to the farm and were always made welcome. Whenever possible we took soap, which was very scarce. They, in return, provided us with many excellent meals.

It was there that I sampled my first *tortilla*, a kind of omelette, to which our hosts added potatoes, onion, garlic, pimientos, aubergines and tomatoes. Bound with eggs and fried in olive oil, it was a most appetising and healthy dish, although perhaps not one that would have been overly popular in the workingmen's cafés around Clapham Junction.

On one of our visits we noticed a chicken with a bandage around its neck pecking away at morsels on the ground.

John and I exchanged glances and our hosts gave us the answer to the unasked question. Yes, the hen we had given them had not died, and they had nursed it back to health.

11 The Sierra Pandols

From our reserve position one evening in mid-August we saw a hill encircled in a ring of flame. It continued to burn for two days. This was the infamous Hill 666 in the Sierra Pandols, a range of mountains south and east of Gandesa. Soon we returned to the line to defend it, taking over from Lister's men.

These Spaniards, under Enrique Lister, had fought with tremendous courage but had been driven away from their line by terrible fire from incendiary shells that had destroyed almost every living thing on the hill. Then, with an almost superhuman effort, the gallant Listers had recaptured the hill and grimly held on.

As we approached the position on a late afternoon, the fascists began shelling us. For the first time I actually saw a shell in the air. This shell had struck the top of the hill we were climbing and ricocheted. We became aware of a huge blurred black mass hurtling towards us. It was accompanied by the sound of a hundred sheets of tin being rattled by a giant hand. Instinctively, I flung myself down and hugged the earth while I waited for an explosion that never came. The shell was a dud.

Franco was now making a desperate effort to force us back across the Ebro and had tremendous quantities of men and war *materiél* behind him, hurriedly drawn from other fronts. As a result the fighting in the Pandols was very severe. Their artillery was exceptionally accurate, literally churning up the ground around us. We saw considerable evidence of the carnage that had taken place.

I was detailed with John Dunlop and my squad of six men to occupy a trench which was over the crest of the hill and thus exposed continually to fascist fire. We had to wait until dark before taking over.

Before leaving the hill, a Spanish sergeant had given us the relevant information about the trench, the barbed wire and the patrolling system in our sector. On a ridge facing us were the fascists at about one thousand metres. The barbed wire entanglements lay some twenty-five metres in front of us and stretched roughly two hundred metres to our left and right. Out in the open to our left was a listening post constructed from a number of large boulders to provide shelter from enemy fire at night.

It was essential that we had at least one man patrolling the wire during the hours of darkness. He was to keep in touch with a patrolman from the Canadians on our left and with one from our own company on our right. On contact, a correct password had to be given and a correct answer received to ensure that all was well.

Immediately we took over from the Listers, I posted a man on patrol and arranged a rota for the night. I shared in this duty and was number four on. The third man had just begun his round when a rifle cracked, followed by a few more, then machine guns and mortars. Hell broke loose.

The patrolman came scuttling back into the shelter of the trench and we all had our rifles on the parapet facing the enemy and waiting for the expected attack. Nothing happened, and after a while the fireworks ceased. It was as if the fascists were formally welcoming us to Hill 666.

Taking stock of our position when it became light, we realised how very high up we were in the Sierra Pandols. The panorama before us was wonderful. Perched there we seemed to be high in the clouds, and from all angles we had a superb bird's eye view of the surrounding countryside. We looked down on rocks, evergreen trees and shrubs. Up in these wild hills the stench of war was masked by the pervasive, aromatic scent of pine and wild rosemary.

About fifty metres to our left something glistened in the early morning sunlight. It appeared to be a pile of cases that had fallen from the back of a mule. The body of the unfortunate animal was sprawled in the grotesque attitude of death. Speculating on the possible contents of these cases and hoping it was food of some kind, we waited impatiently for dusk.

Slowly, ever so slowly, the shadows lengthened until at last it was dark enough to leave the trench. Three of us went forward eagerly to find out what treasures the cases contained. It was fascist ammunition, of the wrong calibre for our weapons, but we carried the cases back over the crest of the hill and handed it over to our colleagues where it would be put to the best use. This was a disappointment as far as the inner man was concerned, but it gave us considerable satisfaction to take anything from the fascists.

The three of us had hardly got back to the trench when the whiz-bangs started. Once again every man was on his toes, prepared for attack. It was nerve-wracking when these exchanges took place at night, for our exposed position meant we would not know if we had been cut from our comrades on either side. The patrolman was our only link, and during these episodes it was always best for him to make for the listening post and stay until the sector quietened down.

On patrol one night, I had traversed the wire both ways, establishing contact with the patrols at either end, and was on my way back in the direction of the listening post. The rough conditions and the monotonous diet of beans played havoc with our digestive systems, and suddenly I knew that I had to answer an urgent call from nature.

Carefully laying down my rifle and loosening my clothes, I squatted in the dark. The fascists chose that precise moment to begin their bombardment. The night air was rent with flashes and explosions and the rattle of machine guns, and I was indisposed in no man's land without cover. Frantically hoisting my trousers with one hand and grabbing my rifle with the other, I ran towards the listening post and threw myself behind the shelter of the rocks. I had been caught quite literally with my pants down.

These nightly 'scares' could not be shrugged off as events without meaning, for each one could well be a prelude to a full-scale attack. Franco was going all-out to throw us back across the Ebro in order to restore his battered prestige, and we had to be constantly alert.

There were periods when a serious attack was expected, and we doubled the guard with two men on patrol at two-hourly intervals. One night my partner on patrol moved off to the right while I patrolled the left, testing the wire every few yards. Reaching the Canadian sector, I waited for their patrolman and, with my rifle at the ready, gave the password. He did not reply immediately so I cautioned him and again asked for the required answer. Once more, he failed to respond. Now thoroughly alarmed, I ordered him to put his hands up. Despite his protests, I took his rifle from him, which I slung over my shoulder, and motioned to him to go forward along the wire in the direction of the listening post. Reluctantly he obeyed, and I followed with my rifle trained on him all the while.

My colleague, who was returning along the wire, realised that something was wrong and rapidly approached us. I told him of my suspicions. After questioning him, my partner was also dissatisfied, so we took him back to our trench and turned him over to John Dunlop.

John examined his papers and plied him with questions and then, to my surprise, shook him by the hand. The man I had encountered in the Canadian sector spoke very little English. But he was in fact genuinely Canadian - a French Canadian, an authentic Mac-Pap with a bad memory for passwords.

Since taking up our positions in the Sierra Pandols we had been engaged only in defence. At last came an order to prepare for a night attack. The main thrust was to be made from a position to the left of our own. We left our trench just after midnight and filed down to the lower slopes of the hill and then further round to the left. From there our approach to the fascist lines would be more of a gradual slope.

The enemy position was on a ridge some eight hundred metres away and, as we waited for the rest of our company to take up their assault positions, we tried to familiarise ourselves with the terrain immediately in front of us. When our eyes became accustomed to the gloom we could make out rocks and gorse bushes that would provide a degree of cover. Our intention was to get as close as possible by stealthy infiltration and then storm on to the final assault. When the signal was given we moved forward, taking care to position ourselves behind the available cover.

All went well and we made steady progress. It was a gentler slope than Hill 481, more favourable to an attacking force, and, as we advanced yard by yard, our hopes were high. Then, suddenly, flashes lit the sky, machine guns spat viciously and the whole front was alert.

Waiting patiently, we held our fire and hoped this was just the nightly 'scare'. But the firing was prolonged and it was clear the fascists were aware of our approach. The element of surprise had failed.

We now returned fire, and as we did so, I had a narrow escape from a bullet in the head. Crouched behind a rock with my rifle protruding through a gap, I was firing in the direction of the enemy ridge. Bullets were flying all around me. I felt, rather than heard a terrific crash, which caused my head to spin. I was certain I had been hit, for my head tingled in a most peculiar way. Running my fingers over my face and head, I was astonished to find no traces of blood. This was truly amazing, and I can only assume that a bullet hit the rock a hair's breadth from where my head rested, causing a startling reverberation. I was very lucky.

The losses were very slight on this attack, but it was impossible to get any closer. With their superior firepower they would have cut us to pieces. We exchanged fire with the fascists until well into the morning, when we withdrew - with some difficulty - to our lines. Thus the only attack we made in this sector ended in failure. We returned to our trench and the routine of defence.

It was a gruelling time for us up in our exposed position. The night patrols were particularly stressful, the fascist mortars highly accurate. And while we were lucky to suffer no casualties among our squad, the company continued to lose men at a depressing rate.

During our time in the trench, I had been worried by an enormous boil on my right forearm. It hurt considerably and needed attention. After twelve unrelenting days in the line we were relieved. Leaving as we had arrived in darkness, we marched back ten kilometres into reserve. A First-Aid post had been set up near our camp, and the next morning I duly reported sick.

A youthful George Wheeler at home in Battersea in the 1930s.

British volunteers before the crossing of the Ebro. Frank West, captured with George in the last action, stands with a Battalion pennant attached to his rifle.

George travelled to Spain in a group led by Jack Jones, seen here in the second row on the left in beret and leather jacket. Jones was badly wounded on Hill 481.

The River Ebro, crossed by the forces of the Spanish Republic on 25th July 1938.

The ruins of old Corbera today, much as they were when George came foraging for food in the summer of 1938.

Hill 481 or the 'Pimple', near Gandesa. Attempts to take this position from the Nationalists resulted in many British casualties.

Lewis Clive at Henley c. 1931. A direct descendant of Clive of India, an old Etonian, Oxford Rowing Blue and Olympic gold medallist, he was killed at George's side near Hill 481.

Lewis Clive in Spain.

In uniform, David Guest, the young Cambridge academic and colleague of George's father on Battersea Council. With him is Harry Pollitt, General Secretary of the Communist Party of Great Britain, who made periodic visits to the British Battalion in Spain. David Guest was killed on Hill 481.

The Sierra Pandols, a mountain range where the British Battalion was involved in bitter fighting during the Nationalist counter attack in August 1938.

The remnants of the British Battalion after withdrawal from the Ebro Front in September 1938. Sam Wild, the Battalion Commander, stands in the centre of the second row with beret and leather coat. Crouching in front of him is Bob Cooney, the Battalion Commissar. 'Hookey' Walker, the Battalion Quartermaster, is third from the right in the second row. George's friend John Dunlop, a tall man in a dark beret, stands at the far right of the back row. A few days earlier George had been taken prisoner.

Two wars in as many years: George in the uniform of the British Army c. 1940.

12 Hospital

The seriously wounded cases had already been sent back across the River Ebro to hospital, and most of those on the sick parade had small wounds, stomach disorders or infections. My arm was now swollen and discoloured and very painful. The medical officer had no hesitation in ordering me off to hospital.

I collected my personal effects from camp and returned to the dressing station to wait for the ambulance. There were six of us: another Englishman and four Spaniards, one a stretcher case.

It was dark when we reached the River Ebro and discovered we were to be rowed over in a large flat-bottomed boat. The other Englishman, a taciturn fellow suffering from a stomach disorder, had no idea where we were. I could only assume we were somewhere south of Mora del Ebro, the point at which we had crossed the river in July.

We helped the stretcher case on to the boat as gently as possible. When we were all seated, the boatman pushed us away from the bank and we glided out into midstream. As I sat there, it all seemed so peaceful and romantic. Small shafts of moonlight played on the water and all was quiet save for the gentle scudding of the oars. How very different was this crossing from the one we had made some weeks earlier in the opposite direction, when Franco's bombers were trying to blast us out of the water.

Slowly we reached the other bank where another ambulance waited. We carefully placed our badly wounded Spanish comrade in the vehicle, found seating for ourselves and then we were off and away from the battle zone. I peered out of the windows to see if I could discern any familiar landmarks. It was far too dark so I tried to snatch some sleep. But sleep came fitfully, for the road was bumpy and the Spaniard periodically cried out in pain. We were all concerned for him and did our best to make him comfortable.

Dawn could not have been far off when the ambulance came to a halt outside the hospital. We were taken into a small reception room and given a mug of hot sweetened milk. At that moment nothing could have been more delicious.

Finishing the nightcap, I was shown to my bed. In the subdued light of the ward, I was overjoyed to see clean white sheets and bedding. But when the nurse motioned for me to strip off and get in, I hesitated: my body was none too clean. This reluctance was only momentary, and I soon nestled down in the luxury of a real bed. I slept soundly.

I was awakened not by bugles, shells or mortars, but by a gentle hand on my shoulder and a woman's voice. Opening my eyes I saw a beautiful nurse offering me milk and bread. I sat up for my breakfast and took in the surroundings. It was much the same as any British hospital might be in wartime. The furnishings and fittings were a little different but there was the same atmosphere of cleanliness and efficiency. I was greeted with friendly nods and gestures from the other patients, most of whom appeared to be Spanish.

My arm was thoroughly examined, prodded and squeezed. The doctor, a young Spaniard who spoke some

English, decided not to lance the boil. Instead, a hefty hot poultice was applied and the arm bandaged. I was told I could get up and go out into the sunshine.

Before I left the ward, I sought out my friendly nurse and asked her if I could have a bath. This she arranged for me and produced scented soap. I was really in luck, and despite the restriction of using only my left arm, that bath must rank as one of my most enjoyable.

I had intended to complete my toilet by removing my beard. But when I saw the reflection in the mirror, it looked too good and I decided to keep it. It was quite a strong beard, gingerish in colour, and I was rather proud of it.

Earlier I had learned we were near the small coastal town of Cambrils. The hospital - originally a college - was a magnificent building standing in lovely and spacious grounds. There were trees in abundance and numerous well-kept flowerbeds. Fruit of all kinds grew there, together with many nut trees. There were apparently no restrictions on picking fruit and I helped myself.

I fell in with a young patient who was very pleased to meet an International Brigader. He was a Lister and had been wounded in the leg during the crossing of the Ebro. He spoke no English, but with the use of signs and the little Spanish I understood, we were able to communicate.

While we were talking a bell rang which, he told me, was the signal for lunch. We walked together to the dining hall. He was on crutches but easily kept pace with me.

The dining hall was a modern structure with large windows through which the sun was shining onto the tables. It had the air of an expensive restaurant, with hospital maids acting as waitresses.

After a first course of soup and crusty bread, plates of fish were brought to the table. These were nicely decorated in circles with the tail of one in the mouth of another, adorned with slices of lemon and accompanied by fresh vegetables. We ate well.

Over lunch my new comrade from the Listers told me his family lived in a small village near Barcelona, and that he was going home on leave the following day. He spoke of the grim military situation but also of his - and his comrades' - resolve to defeat fascism. He made scathing remarks about the British government and non-intervention; remarks I was compelled to endorse rather shamefacedly. We talked for another hour or so and then he had to leave. He shook my hand firmly as he looked me in the eye and exclaimed *"¡No pasaran!"* - They shall not pass!

Walking in the grounds aimlessly after lunch, I pondered on his remarks and wondered about the future. The terrible injustice of non-intervention had come home to me more forcibly than ever. I realised how bitterly anti-fascist these people were, and yet German and Italian planes and tanks could blast their towns and villages without troubling the consciences of the democracies.

My arm still hurt, but after three days of good food, clean conditions and expert medical attention, the pain gradually lessened and the swelling went down. I was on the way to recovery.

During my many wanderings around the grounds, I had discovered a way out of the hospital. This I confided in José, a Spanish patient who slept in the bed to my left. He, too, was not confined to bed, and I asked him if he was 'game' to slip out for a drink. He readily agreed. Discipline was not too severe in the hospital, but we waited until dark and then, like naughty schoolboys playing truant, crept down the corridors and into the grounds, where I led the way to a gap in the fence and the road that led into town.

But we were out of luck. The one café we found was closed, and we resigned ourselves to returning to the hospital. Perhaps we looked thirsty and disappointed, for as we stood in the street two women, who were sitting on a bench outside their home, brought us a glass of wine each. It was a rough white table wine, but after our long walk it was like nectar.

One of the women noticed José's tattered *alpargatas* and insisted he take a better pair that she brought from the house. They fitted him perfectly and, after thanking them profusely, we began to make our way back to the hospital. As we slipped back into the hospital grounds, I reflected on the spontaneous generosity of the Spanish people. They had so little and yet were prepared to share what they had with perfect strangers.

My arm was now rapidly improving and I realised that my brief time away from the frontline was coming to an end. But before I left there was something I had to do. From the top floor window of the hospital I had seen the beautiful blue waters of the Mediterranean. In England I had always been a keen swimmer, and I felt I had to have a dip in the sea before returning to the Battalion.

I started out just after midday. My route was easy as I had orientated myself with my surroundings from the upstairs window. I wandered into the gardens, disappeared behind some tall shrubbery and dashed to the gap in the fence. On the way back into Cambrils I saw two militiamen standing by the roadside. I walked past them without being challenged and headed into town.

With a tall building as a guide, I made good progress. My path took me across fields and through lush fruit gardens. A salty tang in the air indicated the sea was near. Then, as I rounded a bend, a stunning view of the Mediterranean came into sight. Approaching from higher ground, a long line of the coast was visible to me with great rocky groynes that seemed to rise out of the sea and stretch in long arcs to the shore. I stood on a little mound, a wonderful soft breeze flapping my shirt against my body, and gazed awe-struck by the beauty of the scene.

The bandage on my arm was secure and the infection almost cured. Seawater, I reasoned, would help rather than impede the healing process. With the sun high in the sky, I ran down to a beach of white sand, stripped to my underpants and dived into the clearest water I had ever seen.

A group of young lads sporting in the shallows hailed me with the customary "¡Salud!" I returned the greeting and soon they were all eager to speak to a *soldado* from the front. They all had brothers, fathers or uncles fighting in the war and were loudly contemptuous of Franco and his friends.

As they swam with me, they asked many questions, especially when they found I was *inglés* and a member of the International Brigade. But there was one stark question I had to evade:

"When is England going to help us fight the fascists?"

With this innocent reproach echoing in my ears, I walked slowly through the hot afternoon back to the hospital. José informed me the nurse in charge of the ward had missed me. He had covered up for me by telling her I was probably asleep somewhere in the grounds.

"She had a message for you," he said. "You're leaving tomorrow morning."

13 A Stolen Day

There were about fifteen of us in the lorry returning to the front. They were Spaniards mostly and two other International Brigaders: a big genial Swede named Karl Nilsson[36] and a quiet Canadian we nicknamed Mac. Snaking up through the mountains that run parallel to the coast south of Tarragona, we stopped in the town of Tivissa.

The lorry was parked in the centre of the market square and we stood talking in small groups. The Spanish corporal approached Mac, Karl and myself. He told us we could get rations from the *Intendencia*, or supply depot, and suggested we find a local to act as cook. He also had a proposition to make to us.

During the journey from Cambrils, the Spaniards had apparently had a discussion and reached an agreement, and he had come to ask for our approval. It appeared we could wangle a day off by staying in the town for the night and moving off to our battalions the following morning.

Karl, a naturally warm and good-humoured man, gave an expansive grin which indicated his ready assent. Mac shrugged his shoulders and said he was happy with the idea. But my first reaction was one of disapproval. As a newly promoted corporal I felt it my duty to instil discipline, although my rank carried no weight in a mixed unit. The Spanish corporal smiled and cajoled affably:

"Comrade, it's only for a day and besides, who will miss us?"

I am afraid it took little effort on his part to win me over. I could see how keen the others were and had no desire to be a wet blanket. We agreed to meet back in the square at nine o'clock the next morning.

Not unnaturally, our first consideration was food. Karl, Mac and I soon found the *Intendencia*, where we presented our passes and were given rations of meat, dried fish and vegetables. We now had to find a cook.

Outside, my companions seemed distinctly reticent, and many people passed by who might have been willing to oblige. I decided on the direct approach and stopped a middle-aged man in the street. In the best Spanish I could muster, I asked him if he would cook our provisions. He was a short, thickset and rather fierce-looking fellow, and from his appearance, I expected a growl and a blank refusal. Instead, he flashed a toothy smile and invited us to his home.

Señor Gómez was clearly happy to make the acquaintance of three members of the International Brigade, and he proudly presented us to his wife and two daughters. His wife was a short, buxom woman who made us welcome and immediately began to prepare our food. María, the elder daughter, was short and plump and held a baby in her arms. The younger daughter, Julia, did not share the family likeness. She was taller and slimmer and had an irresistible beauty.

María's husband was fighting on the frontline and we learned that Julia was soon to be married to a young man who was also serving in the Republican army. They wanted to know how our forces were faring at the front, and while we tried to be reassuring, we could not hide from them the extreme seriousness of the situation. It was obvious that our offensive, successful though it had been, had now eased up owing to the lack of arms. And Franco, with his German and Italian allies, would be mounting fiercer counter attacks.

Our own rations were but a small supplement to the main meal, and as we sat down to a first course of salad vegetables, I was struck once more by the kindness and generosity of our hosts. We were three foreign soldiers with a basic grasp of Spanish, and yet they treated us like sons and brothers.

After lunch we relaxed with nuts and sweet wine as the afternoon sun streamed in through open windows. Julia and I sat together while I showed her photographs of home. I was the first Englishman she had met and she was curious about England and English life. How very far away it all seemed.

Someone suggested a walk and, to my pleasure, Julia offered to conduct us around the town. So far the war had left no indelible scars on Tivissa. We saw bomb craters and here and there a partially destroyed house. But compared to the other towns I had seen in this part of Catalonia, it was virtually untouched.

Our beautiful guide was obviously proud of her birthplace and delighted in showing us its attractions. Then, as the shadows began to lengthen, Julia insisted the three of us return to her home for an evening meal. Conscious of wartime food shortages, we tried politely to decline, but she was adamant. When we arrived, the table was already laid for us.

Later I sat with Julia on the balcony of her home in the cool of the evening. We watched an electrical storm as it followed the course of a river way off in the distance. With the mountains in the background this was a perfect setting, one that belonged to a soldier away from the frontline. The dirt, the lice and the prospect of sudden death were features of a different world. I was in the clouds with Julia, sitting hand in hand and at peace.

But the evening was all too short and we had to leave. We expressed our thanks to Julia's parents for their great hospitality. Reluctantly I said goodbye to Julia. She too was noticeably reluctant, which made our parting the more painful. Following Karl and Mac out of the door, I walked away into the night.

We made our way to a large barn which we had noted during our afternoon walk. Others had also earmarked the place, for we found many soldiers already camped there. Although warm and cosy in the hay, it was some time before I slept. It was not the snoring of others that kept me awake, but the memories of an incredible evening.

In the morning we found a café and, after breakfasting on dry bread and wine, strolled to the market square. Waiting there in the sunshine for the vehicle to take us back to our units, I reflected on our stolen day in Tivissa, but my heart was heavy when I thought of Julia Gómez.

The morning wore on and there was no sign of a lorry, a driver or the Spanish corporal. As morning gave way to afternoon, we began to have misgivings. It became clear we were destined to spend another night in Tivissa.

So once more we wandered around the town in a quest for food. Mac, the Canadian, decided to go his own way, and I walked the streets with Karl, his good humour and jocularity an antidote to the indecision and uncertainty of the day.

Julia was uppermost in my thoughts and I longed for the sight of her. We could easily have called at the Gómez house, but could not impose on their generosity again, and purposely kept away from their district.

But we were fated to meet again. In the late afternoon, as we turned a corner, Julia and I came face to face. Surprise mingled with pleasure in her eyes as she greeted us and asked why we had not left. She insisted we return home with her, and brushing aside our protests, she linked one arm in each of ours and led us in the direction of her home.

As we neared the house, Karl turned abruptly and, grinning broadly, said something in Swedish and walked on up the road. Aware that Julia and I enjoyed each other's company, he must have read romance in the air and had no wish to play gooseberry. I was elated at the prospect of an evening alone with Julia and made little effort to change his mind. With a cheery wave he was gone. That was the last I ever saw of Karl Nilsson and I sincerely trust he came out of the conflict unscathed.

Julia's family were surprised to see me, but they made me just as welcome as before and I sat down to another generous meal. As we ate, there was much speculation about the missing lorry. I told the family that it was my intention, come what may, to get back to the British Battalion the following day.

Afterwards Julia and I sat on the balcony. There was no attempt by her parents to chaperone us, and we talked of many things, struggling at times with the language difficulty. She was a really beautiful woman and I regarded myself as extremely fortunate to share her company. My enquiries about her forthcoming marriage were dismissed airily with some remarks that suggested it was a family arrangement. It was a clear night and shafts of moonlight fell across the balcony. Time seemed to stand still. But this was only an illusion, for midnight was approaching and I had to leave.

Returning to the barn, the first person I saw was Mac, who stood by the doorway smoking a cigarette. He had not seen Karl, and we assumed he was somewhere in the barn already asleep. Expecting to see him in the morning, I found a comfortable place in the hay and drifted off.

In the morning there was still no sign of Karl. We all made our way to the market square expecting to see the lorry. Once again we were disappointed. And following a roll call we discovered three men were missing: the corporal, the driver and now Karl. We agreed it would be pointless searching for them; our main consideration was to return to our units.

Mac and I decided to walk to Mora del Ebro and contact the army authorities there. We set off on the road out of town with hopes of getting a lift, but there was little traffic about. Mac was uncommunicative and we spoke little. I was preoccupied with thoughts of Julia and quite unaware of the passage of time.

14 Back To The Battalion

Our reckless and foolhardy escapade had misfired slightly, leaving us both with feelings of guilt. As we trudged on, I conjectured on what could have happened to the corporal, the lorry, the driver and Karl.

On we walked and as the terrain became familiar, we knew we were close to the river. Turning a bend in the road a bridge came into view and, as we got near, guards covered us with their rifles and demanded to see our papers. We explained what had happened in Tivissa and were ordered to report to an officer on the other side of the river.

Once again I was crossing the Ebro, this time on foot and on one of the temporary bridges constructed by our engineers. As we crossed I marvelled at how such flimsy structures could carry tanks and trucks. They were in fact our lifelines.

The officer in charge on the other side advised us to wait for an ambulance that would be going part of our way. We travelled for half an hour or so, and were dropped off with directions to the Canadian food kitchen.

It was now almost dusk, and we plodded on with the incentive of food and drink ahead. The occasional whine and explosive crump of a shell reminded us we were close to the frontline. There was not a soul about, and, as we pressed on into darkness, feelings of unease came over us. Having no idea what was happening at the front, it was quite possible we were straying into enemy territory. We decided to wait until dawn before proceeding and moved off the road to a sheltered spot among some bushes. Sleep came fitfully, and it seemed strange to be so close to the front and yet to be totally on our own.

Dawn was breaking when we were woken by the furious barking of a dog. Instantly alert, we crawled on bellies like Red Indians in a Western film towards the source of the noise. We saw a group of Canadian soldiers teasing a large dog. We had spent the night only a few hundred metres from the MacKenzie-Papineau position. It was exasperating to know we had spent a wakeful and uncomfortable night so near to our own lines.

After a hot breakfast of fried bread, sardines and coffee, I shook hands with Mac, wished him luck and set off to find the British Battalion. It was an easy walk, and I soon reached a British kitchen which had had been established in the rear of a partly destroyed farm building. There I was introduced to 'Hookey' Walker[37], the well-known and respected Battalion Quartermaster. Whatever the situation, he could always be relied on to provide a good meal. He advised me to stay at the kitchen until nightfall when I could return to my company lines with the food lorry.

A fresh issue of newspapers had just arrived, and I was able to catch up on the latest news from home. It was encouraging to read of the meetings organised by Labour parties and left-wing groups and the widespread support for the Spanish government, which found expression in gifts of food and clothing. Resolutions from trades union branches expressing solidarity with us were sent to left-wing papers. Reading them, I felt the entire working class was with us in our struggle.

After a lengthy, leisurely session with the newspapers, I lent a hand in the kitchen. As dusk approached I helped to load food canisters on to the lorry, and then travelled in the back to the Battalion lines.

It was good to be back with my friends and comrades. During my absence our company had taken part in one day's frontline action. In a shellburst two men were wounded and one killed. The fatality was Ernie Sim[38], a quiet retiring fellow from Scotland - another valuable life lost in the anti-fascist cause.

John Dunlop, whom I was pleased to see was fit and well, told me the company's principal task was fortification. For the previous three nights the men had been to different sectors of the front, and that evening was to be no exception. Carrying picks and shovels, we marched for about an hour into awkward and exposed positions in the high rocks. We worked all night to reinforce the trenches and defence posts and stopped only as dawn broke.

Exhausted, we marched slowly back to our camp in a long, twisting valley. Because of incessant bombing we were compelled to take refuge in crude dugouts or foxholes.

Each morning we returned to this position after a gruelling night's work, often under shell or mortar fire. Our chief consideration was sleep, but this was achieved in the heat of the day with difficulty. There were swarms of flies everywhere and our clothes ran with lice. Spirits began to sag.

The visits by German and Italian bombers became more frequent, and dense clouds of smoke and dust hung above the valley. We each had a particular foxhole for these raids, usually at the base of a tree, which gave some additional protection.

In open ground there was no cover other than a series of slit trenches. On one occasion I was in the open when the *avión* whistle sounded and I dashed for a trench. I lay flat on my back looking up at the clear blue sky. The old campaigners had given us a tip on how to avoid shellshock. We were advised to bite on a piece of wood during an air raid, and for this purpose we all carried small pieces in our pockets.

I had my 'bite' in my mouth and as the planes released their bombs, I clamped my jaws on it. Suddenly I felt intense heat and saw a wall of flame shoot across the confined space of the trench. The walls of the trench seemed to close together above me, and for a brief moment I had the feeling that I was about to be buried. Just as suddenly the walls sprang back to their original position, and after the planes passed I scrambled out unscathed. Looking to my right, and only a few yards away, I saw a large bomb crater and marvelled at my lucky escape.

There had been a reshuffle of men during my stay in hospital. My own squad now consisted of some old colleagues and new Spaniards[39] who were now serving alongside the international volunteers.

Rumours of a fascist breakthrough were increasing. One morning I was in my dugout trying to snatch some sleep after a hard night on fortifying duty. Sounds of commotion roused me from sleep and I emerged from my shelter to see men rushing in every direction.

I heard someone shout, "The fascists are up there on the next ridge."

Cold panic gripped me, and in the bustle and excitement I felt like running. Fortunately the feeling was only momentary, and grabbing my rifle I concentrated on getting my squad together. Joining up with another section we approached the ridge the fascists were thought to have captured.

On the way up I had a problem with one of my men. A Spaniard, he was the company barber, and was reluctant to move. *"¡adelante!"* - forward! - I yelled, and prodded him from behind with my bayonet, conveniently forgetting that a few minutes earlier I had almost been ready to flee.

We reached the top of the ridge with great apprehension, expecting to be met by a withering fire from the fascists. To our relief and astonishment, we found the ridge was unoccupied. There had been considerable shelling and we had sustained casualties, but no fascists were to be seen.

A young Spaniard had been badly shot up in the stomach, and four of us carried him back in a blanket. We each held a corner and struggled down over rocky ground. He was in desperate pain and called out for water. We had been warned of the danger of giving water to anyone with a stomach wound and had to refuse. His cries were pitiful, and I was more upset by this young boy's agony and fear than by many of the dreadful sights of the previous two months.

15 The Last Action

On September 22nd 1938 we were told we were going into the line again. We were also told that, following this action, the International Brigades were to be withdrawn from Spain[40]. Reminding us of the proud record earned by the British Battalion - the 'Shock Battalion' of the 15th Brigade - our officers were confident we would uphold its splendid name.

With full complement we left the valley and marched to face our final engagement with the enemy. What would be the outcome? Who would survive?

The climb from the valley was arduous, with each man fully laden, but once on the road we made good progress. We marched in darkness, our surroundings illuminated by the moon. The road sloped steadily upward and all around us steep crags seemed to tower menacingly. As we neared the sector of the front which we were to defend, we were cautioned to be as quiet as possible.

There were many tracks leading off from the road, and there was some uncertainty on the part of our officers. Finally halting, it was realised they had blundered and we turned about to retrace our steps. Identifying the correct path to follow, we at last reached our destination. The error had cost us considerable time and it was almost dawn when we reached our positions.

Owing to the confusion, our sections and squads had become mixed. On my left was Frank West, previously the Commissar of No.1 Company[41]. On my right was a

Scotsman called Tommy McGuire[42]. John Dunlop was about twenty metres further down the line.

The trenches were dug in hard rocky soil and in places were less than a metre deep. I was compelled to lie full length as it was now almost light and the fascists began sniping at us.

We could now see how difficult it was going to be to hold this advanced position. To our left was a high hill with almost sheer sides. In front, the hill sloped gently away from us like a giant staircase, the steps being formed by stone terrace walls. To our right was a thickly wooded slope that would give the enemy excellent cover.

Frank West and I set about trying to improve the situation by deepening our trench. Lying full length in a narrow trench trying to wield a pick is tiring work. Wielding one on rocky soil is more tiring still. And when one has had little sleep in days, the task is enervating. We toiled away in an attempt to give us more cover, but made little impression on the unyielding rock. Our efforts became less energetic and we fell back exhausted. As I lay there, clasping my pick, my fingers gradually relaxed their grip, my eyes closed and I sank deep into the oblivion of sleep. The human frame can only stand so much and others had already dozed off.

We were woken by a massive aerial bombardment which was followed by ferocious artillery fire. Those of us in the shallowest trenches could only lie there and hug the earth. The continuous hail of shells prevented us from looking over the parapet and we simply hung on, waiting for a respite. The bombardment seemed to last for hours, and then suddenly it ceased.

A few minutes passed and I heard someone yell: "Look out, they're up here!"

I made a movement to get at my rifle, but the fascists were there with hand grenades held aloft. Shouting *"¡manos arriba!"* - hands up! - they ran along the parapet throwing our rifles out of reach. There was nothing for it but to surrender.

They had exploited the woody slope on our right to perfection, advancing to striking distance under the cover of their murderous artillery barrage. Seven of us were captured. Herded together we were taken back behind enemy lines, and at one point forced to run the gauntlet of our own machine gunners, who fired on us under the impression we were fascists.

We got out of range by scrambling down into a gully, where we sat waiting for the next move by our captors. They were a mixed unit of Spaniards and Italians. The Spaniards wore the red berets and insignia of the *Requetés*[43], notorious fanatical fascists who acted towards us just as we expected. But two of the Italians, probably conscripts in Mussolini's army, behaved more reasonably, offering their cigarettes around and speaking to us without venom or hatred.

There, in the loose earth, I buried my army papers and notes, which I thought might be of use to the enemy. We were then forced out of the gully and shunted further back away from the firing line. Fascists stood and jeered, kicking and slapping us as we came by.

A short, dandified captain appeared and ordered us to be searched. They then robbed us of anything of value.

Wrist watches, rings, fountain pens and wallets were removed. Those of us who had good boots or shoes were forced to exchange them for old *alpargatas*. Our hands were tied behind our back and we were lined up against a rock wall.

16 A Grave For Seven

The captain, clearly enjoying every minute of our discomfort, gave an order for a grave big enough for seven to be dug. We watched them digging while the gallant officer strutted in front of us and prodded us with his stick. My ginger beard conveyed the impression I was Russian. Leering up at me, his face only inches from mine, and hissing, "¡*Ruso, Ruso!*" he jabbed me viciously in the ribs.

We all had similar treatment as he swaggered from one to another. Tommy McGuire was felled by a blow from the captain's stick. With his hands tied behind his back, he managed to gain a kneeling position, whereupon the officer grabbed a pickaxe and began playfully to jab at Tommy's head.

All the while the grave got deeper. The NCO in charge asked the officer if it was deep enough. The captain examined the hole and ordered them to continue digging. He then approached us again. Starting with Tommy McGuire, he raised his arm in the fascist salute and asked:

"¿*Tú quieres esto?*" - you want this? The answer was a distinct and defiant "¡*No!*"

Clenching his fist in the international anti-fascist salute, he again asked:

"¿*Tú quieres esto?*" Tommy's response was a determined and confident "¡*Sí!*"

Leaving Tommy, he came to me. I answered in the same way. And of the seven, only one wavered and gave the bully any satisfaction. The physical and mental strain of the past few days - and the sight of our grave being dug - proved too much for our youngest, a lad of nineteen. He gave a barely audible yes to the fascist salute. This provoked an immediate response from a Scotsman called Jimmy Pollock[44]. In clear and precise Spanish, he told our tormentor that the boy was very young and didn't realise what he was saying. My heart warmed to Jimmy at this, for here was a reaffirmation of our determination to go down as real anti-fascists and a sharp rebuff to this pompous little sadist.

That the end was near, I had no doubt, and a variety of emotions flooded through my mind. There was hate and defiance as I watched the antics of the diminutive fascist dandy who controlled our destiny. There was pride and exultation in the way we had stood up to this contemptible bully. But there was sorrow and worry as I thought of my parents and family. I thought of cycling, swimming and the good times spent with my brother, sister and friends at home in London.

Two fascist soldiers stood with automatic rifles poised, and we waited for them to fire. Another officer appeared and a heated discussion ensued between him and the captain. From what we could gather, the captain wanted to shoot us all while the second officer thought it best to await the verdict of a superior.

It was curiously amusing to watch our fate being decided by these two excited men, who shouted at each other and gesticulated wildly. Eventually the newcomer had his way. We were not going down the hole after all.

17 Marching To Captivity

We were pushed away from the grave and up a rough track that led into a large open field. Other captured International Brigaders joined us, and many more Spaniards, mostly Catalans serving in the international units. Our names and addresses were taken[15].

A group of officers came along, surveying us like cattle. They held a lengthy discussion about us, pointing in different directions. Finally arriving at a decision, we were ordered to fall in and march. We were kept away from the main roads and walked across country using only narrow lanes and cart tracks.

Among the Spanish prisoners were several wounded and we took turns carrying them. One of these died while being carried and when we stopped, and the bearers lowered the stretcher carefully to the ground, two guards came over, swearing, and asked the cause of the delay. They callously tipped the body of our comrade aside and ordered us to march on.

All that day we marched in the sun, with few halts and no water. Several small villages were passed through and the reception from the civilians was far from hostile. In one village there was a well in the square and we halted while the guards refilled their water bottles.

During the march we had kicked up clouds of dust which mingled with perspiration and caked on to our bodies. Dust clogged our nostrils and throats. My beard - bathed in sweat and coated in grime - was particularly uncomfortable.

Now we watched and waited patiently as the guards drank and splashed water around. We dared not break ranks for fear of being clubbed with rifle butts. A group of women standing by saw our plight and went into their houses, returning with pots and pans filled with water, which they offered to us. Those prisoners nearest the houses were lucky enough to enjoy a good swig before a guard came over and, with a roar and a curse, snatched the containers and emptied the water on the ground. Admonishing the women, he ordered us to march on.

As we pressed on the scenery varied from rocky, barren terrain to softer ground with green vegetation. For a short stretch we marched parallel to an irrigation ditch. One prisoner bent down and scooped a handful of water, only to be clubbed for his rashness. I dropped my rather filthy handkerchief into the ditch and picked it up. I was able to moisten my lips but my throat remained parched.

The day wore on and, as the shadows lengthened, the heat from the sun diminished in intensity, and our discomfort eased. But we were still very thirsty, very tired, very dirty and looking forward to some kind of rest. It was then that we stopped outside the wine-pressing establishment on the outskirts of Bot.

18 Bot

"George Wheeler, why did you come to Spain?"

Looking straight into the eyes of my questioner I replied:

"Because I am opposed to fascism."

The officer wrote something on a piece of paper before him and then asked:

"If you were released, would you return to Spain?"

"Very probably."

After making another entry on the paper, he made a signal to the guards and I was led away through the doors. Walking out I was aware of intense brightness, and after the gloom of the wine press I was dazzled. What now, I thought. Where was my executioner? Where was my grave?

I heard a burst of gunfire, but felt nothing and kept on walking, prompted by the guard behind me. We walked to the end of the building and as I turned the corner I was conscious of a great, physical surge of relief. For there were my comrades, apparently in fine fettle. Simultaneously astonished and elated, I took my place in the line and watched the performance as the remaining three came out in turn. When the last International Brigader was out of the building, the bursts of gunfire ceased and the Spanish prisoners were marched out. I reflected on the meticulous care with which the fascists had prepared their sadistic little joke.

A number of lorries were lined up on the road. From one of them, the fascists unloaded several sacks which proved to contain food. Each man was given a tin of stew and a tin of fruit. We were told these rations were to last us for our journey, but not knowing our destination, had no idea how long to make them last.

The guards then herded us into the lorries and we travelled for an hour, all tightly packed together. It was an unsettling time, and I tried to turn my thoughts away from the uncertainty of our future to pleasurable memories of my recent past. I thought of Julia.

Halting at a large wide building we were escorted through the door helped by kicks and the occasional thump of a rifle butt. Our new dungeon was more spacious than our previous accommodation and we assumed it had been a canteen or café, for there was a counter down one side and the walls and floor were tiled.

Two big windows looked out onto a stream. It was early afternoon when we arrived, and most of us took the opportunity to sleep in the sunshine which streamed through the windows. We heard and saw no more of our captors that day.

After a cheerless night trying to sleep on cold, hard tiles, we were bundled on to the lorries and once more treated to a packed, uncomfortable and bumpy ride. The convoy halted in the afternoon to allow the drivers and guards to enjoy a long and leisurely lunch. While they ate and drank outside, we were forced to stay on the lorries. There were loud entreaties from those who needed the use of a toilet. But as we found to our discomfort, our captors derived great amusement in refusing us this basic human right, and made coarse and puerile jokes about our predicament.

19 Zaragoza

It was evident we were travelling westwards into the heart of fascist territory. Early that evening we reached Zaragoza. We were taken to a big old building that, we subsequently learned, had once been a college and now served as a prison. The doors opened and we were pushed into a stone corridor some five metres wide and thirty metres long. The doors closed and we were left on our own.

Our third jail in as many nights had parallels with Bot. But it had one big advantage in the form of a single squat toilet. Cramped and tired as we were, men formed an orderly queue and waited patiently. It was another uncomfortable night, and while everyone remained calm and quiet, I could sense the anxiety in the air.

With the morning came our captors, who ordered the International Brigaders, now more than twenty of us, to fall out. We were led along a series of passageways and then into a large stone-tiled cell. Five metres above the ground was a window with an open fanlight. There were eight other occupants of the cell: four Italians and four Germans. They had been there for four months and two of them were under sentence of death. Fiercely anti-fascist, they remained unbowed and defiant. As a consequence, the guards always entered the cell in pairs and with revolvers.

As darkness approached on our first night in this cell, so it got colder and colder. We had received no more food and were very hungry. We were clad for the summer heat of the Ebro Valley, and were now cold and miserable. My own clothing consisted of a singlet, short underpants, a thin shirt, trousers, socks, sandals and a beret. My colleagues were similarly dressed and the only way we could face the cold was to snuggle together. Lying in a long line, each man pressed close to another, we shivered through the night.

As the first streaks of dawn light heralded the approach of a new day, we got to our feet and began to exercise in an effort to get warm. Walking round and round, up and down, we swung our arms to get the blood circulating. It was not until the sun was well into the heavens that the cell became warm enough for comfort. The German and Italian prisoners had a blanket each and we hoped we would be given one if we were to stay for any length of time.

We stayed there for ten cheerless days and nights. The pattern was the same each day. In the morning we received a cup of lukewarm ersatz coffee. At midday the guards brought small quantities of lentil soup. In the evening we were given a bread roll and, if we were lucky, a sardine. Each afternoon we were pushed outside for an hour's exercise.

No blankets arrived and, with a cold wind whistling around the large stone-tiled cell, the nights were very difficult. We asked if the open fanlight could be closed, but were told it would be unhealthy. The irony was not lost on us.

The only action that broke the monotony of this grim prison was the casual brutality of the guards. One day we watched helplessly as one of the Italians was lashed mercilessly with a stick for some trivial offence. Anyone who did not respond immediately to an order from these thugs was liable to receive a vicious clout from a stick, riding crop or rifle butt.

One morning we were led outside and marched to the railway station. We were issued with two days' rations - a small hard bun and a tin of stew - and escorted into cattle trucks. The truck I entered was a simple rectangular box-like structure with a door and window on each side. There were no seats but there was ample room to sit or lie on the wooden floor. After the icy cold of the tiled floor at Zaragoza this was comfort indeed.

Three armed guards travelled with us. They sat on comfortable chairs with their rifles across their knees and warned us not to approach beyond a certain point. We were confined to this truck for two days and nights, and, once more, no allowance was made for the fundamental needs of the human body. When the train halted at a junction we were able to scramble off for a few minutes. But the guards panicked when they feared the train was about to restart and resorted to the usual methods of coercion. Forced back aboard, we remained in the truck until the journey ended.

For most of the first day the train followed the course of the Ebro. The track ran on high ground and looked down on the river which gleamed like a silver ribbon below us. As the train rattled and jolted along there was little to do but perch by the window and watch the constantly changing vistas. The scenery was exquisite. From the hills above the river we travelled down into dry, flat country. This semi-desert landscape rolled off towards higher hills and mountains which sheltered beautiful fertile valleys.

We passed through several small towns, sometimes halting, sometimes crawling at low speed. At one station we witnessed a sight that should have been shown on all the cinema screens of all the so-called democracies of the world. A whole trainload of Mussolini's troops, resplendent in their blue-grey uniforms, and armed to the teeth came by en route to the front. It sickened us that we were powerless to do anything but look on, knowing that this considerable force would soon be raining death and destruction on our Spanish comrades.

This, we knew, was but one tiny detachment of the enormous forces the fascist powers had poured into Spain. It was obvious to most thinking people that without this help, Franco would have been routed by the people and its legally elected government.

We had tried to counter the hypocrisy of non-intervention, and now - as we faced incarceration in a fascist prison camp - there was ample time for reflection. We realised that the war would be over soon. With the German and Italian air forces pounding them daily, the Spanish people could not hold out much longer. And when Hitler had planted Franco firmly in the saddle, what then?

20 The Concentration Camp

Our train journey came to a halt late on the second day at the city of Burgos. Escorted from the cattle truck at bayonet-point we were hurried along to an old ramshackle bus. We drove through dark, empty city streets into the countryside.

The bus stopped outside a large building. Through the gloom I could make out a pair of massive wooden doors which were opened after a ritual of fascist salutes and the examination of paperwork. We marched into a cobbled courtyard. The guards opened a door and motioned us into what could have been a stable. Against one wall was a pile of sparsely filled straw mattresses. Taking one, I spread it out on the floor and was soon asleep.

Early the next morning I woke to a chorus of discordant sounds, bugles, whistles and raised voices. Stacking the bedding away we lined up for breakfast, no more than a ladle of breadcrumbs mixed with olive oil. Being extremely hungry I ate the sloppy, unappetising mess. As I was to discover, this was to be our staple diet.

The guards then took us through an inner door, across a patio and up a wide, winding staircase to an office. Documentation took place and we were allocated to our respective floors. Half of us went to the upper floor, the others to the floor below.

News had leaked that a new batch of prisoners had arrived and, when the doors opened, we saw that a large gathering had assembled to welcome us. There were many nationalities represented, which reminded me of my early training days in Montblanc. Prominent among us was a large English-speaking section, including British, Canadians and Americans. There was handshaking and backslapping and friendly introductions. Cigarettes were produced and soon there was contented puffing from the smokers who had been without tobacco for many days.

Everyone had so much to say and all seemed to be talking at once, but gradually we settled down and were able to take stock of our surroundings. We were in the concentration camp of San Pedro de Cardeña, formerly a convent which had romantic associations with the famous national hero, El Cid. Some said he built San Pedro, others that he was buried there. The El Cid connection was highlighted by a monumental tableau above the main doors depicting a Spanish soldier on horseback dispatching a Moor with a lance.

In that part of the building which housed the Internationals, there were three hundred and fifty men on each of the two floors. Space was very limited and at night mattresses were lain side by side covering the whole floor. Our arrival added to the congestion.

Maurice Levitas[46], a volunteer from the East End of London, offered to share his mattress with me. We all managed to squeeze in somehow and began to adapt ourselves to life in a concentration camp. We talked late into the night, and our new colleagues warned us of what to expect at San Pedro: unsanitary conditions, poor food and brutal treatment.

A bugle woke us early the next morning and several guards came in to ensure that we all got up. Laggards were soon induced to rise by the application of boot and rifle butt. With our bedding rolled and stored, we formed up in ranks of three for morning roll call. We then marched downstairs.

As we descended, those in front began to run, prompted by the shouting and swearing of a sergeant who stood waiting below, swinging a loaded stick. This was 'Tanky', of whom we were warned the previous evening. My first impression was that he was raving mad. He stood there swinging his stick at each man as he passed.

"*¡Venga, hijos de puta, rápido!*" - Come on you sons of whores, quickly.

As I tried to dodge past him I received a vicious swipe on my buttocks. Stinging with hurt and indignation, I hurried to join the others who were forming into ranks further along.

Another sergeant took over and marched us along a well-worn path to Mass. This took place in the open air on a big rectangular patch of ground. At one end stood the priests' cottages. To the left was a high wall against which we were assembled. At the far end was the church building, part of which was known to be used as a storehouse for shells and munitions, and was always closely guarded. Facing us on the other side of the rectangle was a raised platform of earth that supported tables bedecked with coloured cloths and the adornments of the Catholic service. All around us and spaced at regular intervals were guards with rifles and fixed bayonets.

After a while a priest emerged from his cottage and, followed by his attendants, walked slowly along the path and on to the dais. Immediately in front and below of him were Spanish garrison troops and Headquarters staff.

The service began, which we were compelled to attend regardless of our beliefs. Watching the performance, with its gaudy vestments and dreary singsong chants, evoked only boredom. The hypocrisy of the service was so evident, if only because the majority of us were still smarting from Tanky's loaded stick. Any serious attempt by the fascists to arouse interest or enthusiasm had to be doomed to failure from the start, and we could only assume our enforced attendance was in the nature of a punishment.

With the service over, the priest showered his praises on General Franco and told us how evil it was to oppose him. Then the Camp Commandant took over and poured his vituperations on the enemies of Franco. Adopting a military stance, he flung his arm aloft in the fascist salute and began to sing the fascist anthem 'Cara al Sol' - Face to the Sun. The troops joined in before enacting the ritual which terminated all their parades.

The Commandant puffed himself up to his full height, stabbed his right hand into the air with fingers outstretched and screamed:

"¡España!" - Spain! "¡España!" echoed the soldiers in front of him.

"*¡Una!*" - One! - cried the commandant. "*¡Una!*" they repeated.

"*¡Grande!*" - Big! - he cried. "*¡Grande!*" came the response.

"*¡Libre!*" - Free! - he prompted. "*¡Libre!*" they yelled.

And with a massed "*¡Viva España!*" - Long Live Spain! - the parade was over.

We were also expected to take part in these theatricals, to salute when they did and to repeat the promptings of the Commandant. The sergeants and other guards were always among us to try and enforce obedience. But we were very bad pupils and seemed unable to get the hang of the fascist salute. Our arms and fingers seemed reluctant to stretch, which meant our efforts were nearer the clenched fist salute of the Popular Front.

After the parade, we were marched back to our quarters to receive our breakfast of one ladle of bread soup. It was made of stale bread and table scraps, stewed and mashed up with water and olive oil. It looked like pigs' swill. Those of us with strong stomachs ate; others simply couldn't take it.

Most prisoners had an enamel plate and a spoon, and after the swill I joined the washing up queue. There were three hundred and fifty men on our floor and the only water available came from a dripping tap in one of the three toilet cubicles. Waiting my turn in the line, I had plenty of time to take stock of the toilet facilities. At the end of a stone-floored area measuring some fifteen metres by ten metres, there were three cubicles, none with a door. One contained the dripping pipe for which we were queuing. The other two housed continental-style squat toilets with two raised foot blocks on which to balance.

A central drain was designed to remove excrement with the aid of a water flushing system. But as I was soon to learn there was no water, and human waste was piled disgustingly high. We would have to ignore the stench, filth, discomfort and the ignominy of being on full view to others. This was no place for the squeamish.

After cleaning my plate I washed my breakfast down with a plateful of cool water and returned to see what was happening in our quarters. A team of eight men were cleaning the area. This was our only chore in the prison and the duty was worked out alphabetically.

An internal system of guard duty had been devised in which one prisoner was on duty on each floor at two hourly intervals. This was to ensure that escapes were not attempted, for the duty men would be held responsible and punished. The rota came around once in every eight or nine weeks.

Prisoners were allowed to write home twice a month, providing they had the cost of postage. Many were in contact with their families and received money that enabled them to buy cigarettes, chocolate, tinned milk and biscuits. These goods were bought from the *Economato*, a type of co-operative store run by a group of prisoners under the direction of the camp authorities.

Having no money for stamps, I was unable to send a letter home, but each time the mail went out, a few lines were smuggled in a comrade's letter. I was fairly confident that one of them would get through and I would be able to establish contact with home.

Around midday we were marched downstairs for our second meal of the day, which consisted of two small rolls and a ladle of badly cooked beans. The rolls I put in my trouser pocket while I walked around eating the beans. It was the procedure to walk around full circle back to the pots in the hope of getting a second dip if there was any left. The bread rolls I planned to eat later in the afternoon, but I lacked the will power, and by the time we returned for the evening ladle of beans I was starving. Generally the amount of food we received was inadequate, and we were constantly hungry at San Pedro.

Practically each day we had some contact with Tanky. He was a dapper little dandy, a pretty boy with dark curly hair and a well-trimmed moustache. A ladies' man. There were many stories about him, some based on rumour, some on fact.

His hatred for the International Brigades seemed to stem from the time when he served in a tank regiment and received a wound to his leg, which left him with a permanent limp. This came during a brush with the International Brigade and he could never forget it. As is often the case with a small man given a little authority, he was a bully who took delight in beating a man with a stick or club, knowing his victim was powerless to defend himself. He was a thoroughly detestable little man whom I hated from the moment I saw him.

I began to settle down to the routine at San Pedro and to adapt to the conditions. One small trick I discovered was how to evade Tanky's stick when we ran past him on the stairs. As he stood there shouting at us, I ran as if to pass a few feet from him, but at the last minute swerved closer to him. The result was that he lost his aim, and instead of clouting me with the full weight of his loaded stick, he either missed completely or just hit me with his forearm. By the time he recovered his balance, I was away and he was concentrating on his next victim.

My beard, of which I had been so proud, went within days of arriving at the camp. Barbers came every four or five days and shaved us clean and cropped our heads. This was done for reasons of hygiene, but we were never free from lice which bred in our clothes. The seams of our clothes were full of lice and eggs, and as much as we tried to eradicate them with lit cigarette ends, water and patient picking, the repulsive creatures multiplied.

After two weeks at the camp our group of newcomers was summoned to the office. There we were issued with new uniforms similar to those worn by the fascists. We each received a white cotton shirt, a pair of pantaloons, a thin cotton jacket, a pair of socks and a pair of boots, the soles of which were stamped 'USA 1917'. We looked ridiculous and nothing fitted, but the feel of clean clothes was refreshing and for a few days we were free from lice. Without soap and hot water it was impossible to prevent them returning and we were soon as lousy as ever.

One afternoon I was in the long queue at the water pipe patiently waiting to wash my plate. There was a little jostling, inevitable in a crowded place. The man in front suddenly spun round, pushed me and swore in Spanish. I returned the compliment. Realising that a fight was brewing, the others drew back to give us space.

My opponent, whom I later discovered was a good Cuban heavyweight boxer, came at me in a workman-like stance. I squared up to him. The floor, awash as usual with urine, was slippery. The soles of my American army boots were reinforced with metal segments, and each time I tried to lead with my left, I slipped. We became locked in a clinch and fell to the ground.

We rolled and grappled and soon our clothes were soaked in urine. Watching the scene, our colleagues realised we were merely letting off steam and let us wrestle in the filth. It was only with the approach of Tanky that we were pulled apart. No harm was done and we parted without rancour. The following day my new clothes dried out to reveal enormous white stains. I was not a pretty sight, even by the sartorial standards of San Pedro.

21 Fascist Fun And Games

The task of marching us to and from Mass, meals and exercise and for maintaining camp discipline was shared by three sergeants: Tanky, Navarro and the 'Frog'.

Tanky, the deranged fop, was a bully and was hated by everyone.

Navarro was a soldier, apparently without an axe to grind. He carried out his orders conscientiously and efficiently and treated us well.

The Frog was short and paunchy with a fat, bloated face and a weak receding chin. He wore an enormous pair of spectacles from behind which two large eyes blinked out at the world. He shared Tanky's hatred of the International Brigade and, like Tanky, was very brave when armed with a loaded stick and surrounded by his armed guards.

The camp authorities thought we would benefit from exposure to fascist propaganda and required an English-speaking person for a reading. Lining us up, the Frog asked for an *inglés* to step forward. It was amusing to watch the dilemma of the fat little fascist in his endeavours to find a single prisoner who spoke English.

He began to bluster and threaten, but still nobody moved forward. Gradually, losing control of himself, he strutted among us and approached a tall Brigader.

"Where do you come from?"

"Wisconsin" came the reply.

His knowledge of geography was clearly limited, for he moved on to another prisoner. Snorting with rage, he repeated the question.

"Winnipeg" came the monosyllabic response.

Now visibly shaking with temper, he asked me where I came from.

"Battersea."

It was gratifying to see the little tyrant completely nonplussed. And it was clear he was afraid to question us further for fear of compounding his lamentable ignorance. He floundered about until another NCO arrived with a list of names. Conferring together, they selected a name and called a prisoner forward. There was a glint of triumph in the Frog's saucer-like eyes as he handed the man a pamphlet and ordered him to read to us.

It was banal stuff, full of lies and innuendo. But after reading two or three lines our comrade transformed the event into a comedy turn. By reading past full stops and commas and pausing in inappropriate places, he made utter nonsense of it all. We roared with laughter at each misread sentence. Once more the Frog was perplexed. Surely this was supposed to be serious. Why were they laughing?

Not understanding a word, he began to believe the content of the pamphlet was meant to be amusing. His fat face creased into a semblance of a smile and he started to laugh. The other NCOs and guards followed the Frog's lead, and when we laughed they laughed.

One day the Frog informed us that we had to fill in a questionnaire. Each man would then be interviewed separately. The questions dealt mainly with drinking and sexual habits, and were devised in such a way that the answers would inevitably create the impression the International Brigade was composed largely of drunks, sex maniacs and morons.

When my turn came to be interviewed I was taken into an office and told to sit at a large desk. Two officers sat opposite with books and papers in front of them. Without introduction, one abruptly asked:

"Who was Tinker Fry?[47]"

I told them that I did not know. And I still don't. They conferred in Spanish and the second officer scribbled an observation on my paper. Then just as abruptly, he said:

"Name the planets in the solar system."

I had some knowledge of astronomy and promptly named them without hesitation:

"Mercury, Venus, Earth, Mars, the Asteroids, Jupiter, Saturn, Uranus, Neptune and Pluto."

"Pluto?" queried an officer.

"Pluto" I repeated. "Discovered in 1930 by the American astronomer Clyde Tombaugh."

The officers had been checking my answers in a manual they had before them, and it was evidently out of date. I was elated to have scored one over them. There were no more questions.

22 Chess And Boxing

In the harsh and monotonous environment of San Pedro it was important to stay physically and mentally active. Fellow prisoners organised classes and discussion groups. It was possible to learn a foreign language or attend lectures in subjects ranging from history and philosophy to economics and mathematics.

While our captors wished to present us to the world as creatures of low mentality and bestial character, the reality was precisely the opposite. I found myself in the company of men of the highest intellectual achievement, and for many of us who had had to leave school early, the camp took on aspects of a university.

Chess was very popular, and there were always games in progress. The sets were all hand carved from odd bits of wood, some to a very high standard of decoration. An American prisoner called Hyman Wallach[48], who had been a prominent competitive player in the United States, gave a series of lectures and played over famous games from the past. To hear him talking - in our squalid surroundings - with such knowledge about a game once played by Napoleon on the island of St. Helena, was an uplifting and inspiring experience.

I exercised my mind with chess and tried to keep my body in shape with boxing. An enterprising comrade made boxing gloves from old scraps of blanket and we set up a ring at one end of our floor. In my first bout I went three rounds with a Canadian lumberjack. He was shorter than me but powerfully built and gave me some trouble. But with my longer reach I was able to keep him off, and with a series of long leads to the head I prevailed. To my surprise and pleasure, the man who unfastened my gloves was my former adversary in the washhouse, the Cuban boxer.

"*¡Muy bien, hombre, muy bien!*" - very good, man, very good! - and he slapped me on the back. From then on we were the best of friends.

I did my best to stay fit, but the poor food, bad sanitation and lack of exercise caused skin ailments - mainly sores and ulcers - among some of our less active comrades. It was with relief that we heard of the arrival of a representative of the British government. He was a Colonel Martin, and he came on to our floor us and saw our appalling living conditions. Commiserating with us, he assured us he would get medical supplies and soap and towels, and that our conditions would rapidly improve.

He was a government official - a Tory - but nevertheless an Englishman, and we felt he would not fail us. I was worried about my parents and had no idea whether they had received a message from me. I regarded the Colonel's presence as a heaven-sent opportunity to get word to them. I wrote my name and address on a piece of paper and approached him. He was surrounded by other prisoners who were besieging him with questions, but I pushed my way forward and told of him of my concern for my parents.

He gave me a good hearing, took the paper and placed it in his wallet and gave me his solemn assurance that he would personally see to it that my parents were informed I was alive and well. Colonel Martin had given his word as an Englishman and a gentleman and I no longer had to ask my comrades to smuggle my notes in their letters home. My parents would soon know I was in good health and needed only to be patient.

Later I was to discover what a fool I had been to trust Colonel Martin. My parents received no communication from him or the British government. Meanwhile, in the camp, we waited for the fulfilment of his promises. Weeks passed and all we received was an inadequate supply of soap. No medical supplies arrived and our living conditions actually became worse.

Rumours were constantly circulating around the camp. Some were of an optimistic nature, suggesting we were to be released. Others, the gloomy kind, predicted we would all be shot. Most stories were treated with a certain amount of derision but one persisted, with an echo from the Great War: we would all be home by Christmas.

Our prospects, although far from rosy, did at least point to us getting home eventually. But the future looked very black for our German and Italian comrades. What would be their fate when the war ended - as seemed certain - with a fascist victory?

23 Escape

Upon rising one morning, we lined up for the usual head count. The NCOs checked the numbers on our floor and then went to the floor below. Tanky was the sergeant of the guard and he came rushing up in a mad panic. They counted us again and again. Officers appeared with lists of names and a complete roll call began. Prisoners were missing.

Tanky was livid. Our faces betrayed amusement at his tantrums and he lashed out ferociously with his stick. He walked up and down the line pouring abuse at us in Spanish. Six Germans had escaped, he told us, and some of us had helped them. He demanded to know who had assisted the escapees. If nobody came forward, life would go badly for us. We stood there for hours. No one gave any information and Tanky's stick worked overtime.

The prisoners who were on internal guard duty were questioned and cross-questioned and then taken to the guardroom where they were savagely beaten. One of them, a Scot called David Kennedy[49], returned with his back a raw mess.

From then on it was a reign of terror.

When held prisoner for a long period in foul circumstances, it is interesting to observe how men try to make their living areas as homely as possible. In San Pedro a nail from which to hang a spoon was a precious commodity. Most of us had some sort of rack or shelf made from pieces of cardboard or wood to house a plate and mug. Some prisoners fared better and built small cupboards in which to house photographs and letters. It all helped to restore some sense of order in an otherwise chaotic situation. But with the escape of our German comrades and the consequent terror, the fascists took the opportunity to humiliate us further.

One night Tanky and his henchmen came rushing up to our floor shouting and swearing. He told us that someone had a knife hidden and there would be a search. There was no knife, and we all knew that, but the guards went round the walls tearing out racks, shelves and cupboards. Cups, plates and spoons were thrown to the floor in a mock endeavour to find the knife. The patient work of weeks was destroyed in moments.

This petty and spiteful performance was repeated again and again. There was a rumour that Tanky had been severely reprimanded for being absent from his post on the night of the escape and had been seen at a local dance. Whether true or not, this pathetic man became more of a tyrant and bully than ever before.

Many of the NCOs took Tanky's lead and would appear in our quarters in the early hours of the morning, obviously drunk. They would hurl abuse and provoke us, hoping for a show of anger or resentment that would justify a vicious clubbing.

Following the escape, the commandant ordered the internal prisoners' guard to be trebled. We were warned that any further escape attempt would result in severe punishment for the internal guard, with the clear implication that they would be shot.

We waited eagerly for news of the Germans, and as the days passed and nothing was heard, we had high hopes. Then came bad news. They had been recaptured, just three kilometres from the French border. This was a bitter blow and a noticeable air of gloom descended on the camp.

About a week after recapture the six unfortunates were brought back to San Pedro. We heard many tales of the terrible vengeance of the officers. These poor young anti-fascist Germans were savagely beaten and we never saw or heard from them again.

24 A Brush With Tanky

After the episode with the German escapees, we expected our captors' perpetual persecution would ease up, but we expected too much.

Periodically we were marched to the area where Mass was held. There we would be put through pointless exercises in drill. The NCOs would amuse themselves by ordering us to remain on the spot while they issued staccato commands:

"Right Turn...Left Turn...About Turn...Half Right Turn..."

With several turns in rapid succession we invariably became giddy and lost our balance. This then gave them the excuse to get at us with their sticks.

Tiring of this fatuous game they would have us salute the flag. We were compelled to stand to attention and copy the sergeant. On his command we had to raise and lower our right hands in the fascist salute. We were clearly inept and found it difficult to unclench our fists. At the same time we were to shout "Franco!" This was to be chanted rhythmically and in two distinct syllables:

"Fran-Co!"

With volume and enthusiasm we English-speaking prisoners shouted "Fuck You!" The guards would come in among us swishing their sticks and yelling *"¡mas fuerte!"* - much louder. And with even greater gusto we would respond with "Fuck You!...Fuck You!"

Some days there would be no drill at all and we were allowed to sit and read or exercise as we wished. Since the escape attempt, security had been tightened throughout the camp. A new rule forbade us from walking within metres of the church doors, behind which munitions were rumoured to be stored. One afternoon a boisterous game of football was in progress and I moved away from the noise to read in relative peace.

Concentrating on my book I took no notice of a warning shout. I became aware of a hush, and looking up I realised I had inadvertently strayed beyond the prescribed boundary. Coming towards me at speed was the ridiculous figure of Tanky, his loaded stick raised. I scrambled to my feet and began walking back to my comrades.

Within moments Tanky was upon me and began to belabour me across the buttocks, back, shoulders and head. He would have dearly loved to see me run, but out of sheer cussedness I would not give him the satisfaction. I would have loved to have turned on him and given him the thrashing he deserved, but to do so would have invited the bullets of his watching associates. On I walked at a steady and even pace as the diminutive maniac kicked and swiped and swore.

My comrades made a quite a fuss of me when I reached them and attended to my cuts and bruises. Tanky had hurt me, but I had kept my head up and, in the opinion of my fellow prisoners, I had won a distinct moral victory.

25 Christmas 1938

Our reading material was rather limited: a few books that were passed around and scraps of newspapers which we avidly read and discussed. But we were fortunate to have with us a prolific writer who kept a constant stream of cowboy, adventure, love and comedy stories flowing from his pen

His name was Nick Elendiuk[50], a Canadian cowboy who wrote under the nom-de-plume of Wasylovitch. A big, cheerful chap with a wonderful sense of humour, his stories were read and enjoyed by all the English speakers. It was not unusual for dozens of pages to be passing from hand-to-hand long before the story was finished. And there sat Nick, with his vivid imagination, writing away to keep us interested and amused.

It was now well into December and the optimists among us grudgingly conceded that any hopes of repatriation by Christmas were forlorn. We would have to enjoy the festival as best we could. A committee was set up to organise a concert and prisoners were asked to contribute.

One by one the different nationalities received Christmas gifts from their anti-fascist organisations at home. The Americans received cash. The French received a few parcels containing cigarettes and chocolate. The Swiss were also lucky. There was nothing for the British.

Two or three days before Christmas the Canadians received a few *pesetas* each, but still the British were the poor relations. Surely with all the anti-fascist activity at home we were not to be forgotten.

On Christmas Eve Nick Elendiuk put his hand on my shoulder and invited me to share a snack. With his *pesetas* he had bought a bar of chocolate and a packet of biscuits. He scraped the chocolate on to an enamel plate and added water. He placed the plate over an old milk tin that contained a small piece of candle. When lit it gave off sufficient heat to boil our chocolate which, together with the biscuits, provided a wonderful feast. The comradeship he showed by sharing his Christmas gift registered with me and I felt proud to be his friend.

That night my thoughts were back home in Battersea with my family, and I wondered if I would ever see them again. That their thoughts were with me I had no doubt, and with the hope that Colonel Martin had informed them of my safety and good health, I felt a little reassured. As I was to learn, the silence and indifference of the Colonel led to months of worry and anguish for them.

Christmas morning came with the usual chase down the stairs and Tanky's habitual kicks and cuffs and verbal abuse. Breakfast was the same breadcrumb and olive oil slop. We washed our plates and cleaned our quarters as we would on any other day. And then a rumour started: downstairs there were boxes of goods for the British prisoners.

Three large wooden crates were brought upstairs and we formed up in single file to receive our share. Our friends at home had really served us well, and each man received packets of cigarettes and biscuits, chocolate, toffees, figs, apples and oranges. It was an excellent Christmas present, timed to perfection, and from being the poorest we were now the better off.

That evening we were led to a large indoor hall area for the Christmas concert. The Commandant and officers sat in specially prepared seats while the prisoners stood or sat on the floor. I marvelled at the talents revealed that night. Men with whom I had been incarcerated for months proved to be gifted singers, dancers, storytellers and comics. It was wonderful entertainment. Nick Elendiuk sat with me on the floor, and I was able to repay his earlier generosity with interest.

But the spirit of Christmas only extended so far. The camp authorities were determined the concert would not be a cover-up for an escape attempt. The day devoted to peace on earth and goodwill to all men ended with kicks and slaps from our captors as we were herded back to our floors for the nightly roll call.

26 Leaving San Pedro

As the New Year approached news filtered in of a big fascist offensive in Catalonia. Reluctantly we had to admit the war was almost over. The air of despondency was now very apparent, and it contrasted sharply with the vindictive cockiness of the sergeants who never let up in their acts of petty spite.

On New Year's Eve there were no celebrations. Our thoughts were mainly of home - and if and when we would get there.

In the middle of January came the first real move. Our eleven Swiss comrades were ordered below for haircutting and shaving. This was something new as we were given our tonsorial treatment in no prescribed order. We eagerly waited for them to return and were elated to hear they were leaving the following day.

Speculation was now rife. A week went by - a week of excitement and expectation. And then one morning came the order we had all been waiting for:

"*Todos los ingleses abajo*" - all the English downstairs.

Emotions ran high as we were inspected by officers and given newer uniforms and boots. We were cropped and shaved and then ordered back upstairs to collect our few belongings. Many friendships had been made in San Pedro and men rushed from floor to floor to shake hands and bid farewell. We were finally leaving.

There were seventy-seven British prisoners, together with thirty-one Canadians, and we formed up in ranks. The gates opened and we marched out under armed guard. Tanky stood and leered as we passed.

As we rounded a bend, marching along in high spirits, San Pedro de Cardeña and our stunted fascist tormentor were lost to view. We began to sing, and our songs soon became revolutionary songs. The guards, unaware of what we were singing, encouraged us to continue.

Our destination was Burgos and we marched for what seemed like hours. Many of us had tried to keep fit in San Pedro, but after months of enforced idleness and poor food, this vigorous and sustained exercise was beginning to tell. The pace began to slow. Then, after turning a corner, Burgos was at last in sight.

We now marched with verve and, before entering the city, word was passed along the ranks to smarten up and show the fascists how to march. We entered Burgos more like a victorious army than abject prisoners of war.

The guards led us to the railway station and on to a platform where a train waited. We were pushed into cattle trucks identical to those that had carried us from Zaragoza to Burgos. Our truck had evidence that the previous occupants had actually been cattle, and we had the prospect of a long, uncomfortable and smelly journey. But who cared? We were homeward bound. Or so we thought.

27 San Sebastián

The train terminated in the railyards at San Sebastián in the Basque country. After a roll call to check we were all present, we marched through the city towards the provincial prison.

People began to follow us, and on reaching the main thoroughfare, men and women surged around us in what we feared was a hostile demonstration. But it was nothing of the sort. Cigarettes and fruit were passed to us and we saw one or two surreptitious clenched fists. It was clear these civilians were for rather than against us, and they kept up beside us on the pavements.

The prison was on the seafront. Through the crowd of people I could see white sand and the wide blue sweep of the bay. Massive gates swung open and, as we passed through, the demonstration dispersed.

We found ourselves in a massive forecourt. Guards and warders were everywhere.

Iron staircases led to balconies five storeys high. On the balconies were men in blue overalls whom, we discovered later, were good conduct prisoners responsible for food distribution and cleaning duties.

Lining us up in rows, the guards ordered us to strip and place our clothes and possessions in front of us. These were thoroughly searched and anything deemed suitable as a tool or weapon was confiscated. Our names were called in turn and, as a final ignominy, we had our fingerprints taken like common criminals.

Putting our clothes back on, we were led to a stone staircase in the corner of the forecourt and down to a complex of cells in the basement. Linked by a series of corridors, the individual cells measured no more than three metres by two metres, with a toilet in one corner and a water tap in the other. The doors were left open.

We made the grim discovery that some of the cells were occupied by the Swiss prisoners who had left San Pedro before us. They gloomily explained that negotiations for release had broken down and prophesied we would be there for months. In the dim subterranean light, they told us that the food and conditions were even worse than San Pedro.

So far there were only one hundred and ten men in the basement, which worked out at roughly four to a cell. In each cell was a hole in the ceiling where the water pipe came down from the floor above. Through these holes we were able to converse with the Spaniards in the cells above and we learned a lot about the prison.

It held hundreds of prisoners, many of whom were captured in the early days of the war. We learned there were women with babies imprisoned in San Sebastián, forced to eat the same awful food as the rest of us. We were told of a priest who was ordered by the fascists to broadcast the 'truth' about the bombing of Guernica. When he refused to read their lies over the radio, he was clapped in San Sebastián with a death sentence over him.

In the mornings we were served a thin brown liquid that masqueraded as coffee. Those who drank it did so mainly because it was warmer than the water from the tap. At midday we had a few lentils and a small roll. In the evenings we received a mixture of cods' heads stewed in oil and water. It was a greasy, sloppy mess with small bits of meat clinging to fishbones and here and there an eye. At first my stomach revolted, but the longer we stayed at San Sebastián the more I began to enjoy it. Fish eyes became a delicacy.

Initially I shared a cell with two of the British prisoners captured alongside me in the last action. Frank West was a pithy, laconic Londoner. He had had cooking experience in the past and would amuse us by pretending to prepare a meal in full and delicate detail. Charlie Matthews[51], also from London, was no mean artist, and would draw the finished meal on the wall opposite. He had managed to procure some coloured crayons and after a few weeks we were surrounded by the most exquisite culinary murals.

Each day more prisoners were brought in and our cells began to fill up. Four comrades from the Asturias moved into our cell. They were bitter, hardcore anti-fascists who swore to us that they would devote the rest of their lives to the overthrow of Franco and his regime.

Their presence greatly improved communication with the Spaniards above. One morning they told us that a youth of nineteen, who had been a prisoner for fifteen months, had been taken out in the night and shot. Events like that often happened. There were nearly one hundred men under sentence of death in San Sebastián, two of them in the cell above.

As the days wore on our hopes of release began to fade. Spanish prisoners continued to arrive and the basement cells filled to capacity. There were no books, no chess and few opportunities for exercise. I tried to keep fit by sparring with Nick Elendiuk and running along the corridors, but this became impossible as the overcrowding became worse.

Towards the end of February a strong rumour persisted that we, the Internationals, would soon be leaving. Each day the rumour gained strength. At the end of the month the British prisoners were ordered to assemble in the main basement corridor.

There was great excitement as an official appeared with a sheaf of papers and began to call out names. Slowly, methodically, the names were called in alphabetical order. As each man was called so he moved to the other side of the corridor. The other nationalities watched with interest, and no doubt a little envy, as we prepared for our release.

Slowly, ever so slowly, the names were called. How I wished the official would hurry. Why was I called Wheeler and not Aaronovitch? The official reached the initial 'S', folded his papers and stopped. He stood there while the guards checked and double-checked. Exactly sixty-seven men were to be released, leaving behind ten Britons, thirty-one Canadians and eleven Swiss. What a disappointment for those of us left behind. What a blow. And why only sixty-seven? We never did find out.

Since arriving at San Sebastián we had had no soap or towels and our only recourse was to hold our heads under the cold-water taps and scrub with our hands. We dried off with our shirts, which were by now black. Body lice returned to plague us.

It was now March and the weather was freezing. We, the lucky ones, had blankets which we wore around our shoulders like ponchos. With the cold, the poor food, the lice and the lack of exercise, we were really up against it.

Then one morning we woke to the sound of water pouring into the cell. To our dismay we discovered it was not water but urine and excrement overflowing from the toilet. It was the same in every cell and, as the plumbing fault became evident to the authorities, we were ordered upstairs to the forecourt.

We were compelled to stay there all day while plumbers worked to repair the drains. After a mighty mopping-up operation, we were allowed back into our cells for the night, only to taken out again in the morning. This continued for six days, during one of the coldest spells I have ever known. It began to snow and continued to snow. We walked up and down, stomping our feet, flapping our arms. It was torture.

28 Release

March dragged slowly by. At the end of the month the fascists entered Madrid. The war was effectively over.

On the morning of April 5th 1939 the remaining Canadian, Swiss and British prisoners were ordered upstairs to be shaved. We were to be released, and this time it was for real.

When the big iron gates finally opened and we walked out into the open, I felt intoxicated. The bay looked beautiful and everything around me seemed to sparkle. My brief reverie was interrupted by the curt commands of the guards, and I joined my comrades to scramble into the waiting coaches. We sped towards the French frontier. Passing through Irun we saw evidence of the heavy fighting that had taken place here earlier in the war.

Alighting at the International Bridge, we waited tensely while the formalities were completed. Then, as the big iron barricade bar swung up, we marched across and on to friendly French territory proudly singing the *Internationale*.

Representatives of the British and French governments were waiting for us. They directed us to the public washing baths where we enjoyed steaming hot baths. For the first time in months I revelled in what is normally commonplace - the feel of soap and hot water on my body. It was ecstasy.

A representative of the Canadian government arrived and provided us all with new clothing. Fresh underclothes, socks, new shoes and blue overalls replaced the rags of San

Sebastián. As a further treat we were taken to a restaurant for a real meal of roast beef, potatoes and green peas. I drank wine for the first time since my time with Julia and her family in Tivissa.

After a medical examination and a series of inoculations, we were ready for the long journey home. But before we started, there were papers to be signed. We had to promise to pay back to the government the cost of our repatriation[52].

From the British we received nothing but the prospect of an invoice. The Canadians, however, excelled themselves, and on the train northwards, they conveyed to us from the restaurant car supplies of bread, butter, eggs, fruit and chocolate.

At Bayonne we parted company with the stalwarts of the Mackenzie-Papineau Battalion, who were going on to Le Havre. Living with and suffering the adversities of incarceration together, firm friendships had been formed among us. I shook hands with Nick Elendiuk and felt true emotion. He was a prince of fellows.

The train carried us through the fresh, green countryside of France. As I looked through the window at these gentle landscapes, with hedgerows full of spring flowers and trees newly in blossom, my thoughts returned to the harsh and unyielding terrain of Hill 481 and the Sierra Pandols. I thought of Lawrence Pryme and Lewis Clive and David Guest and Ernie Sim: comrades and friends who now lay beneath the rocky earth of Spain.

I thought too of the song we sang as we advanced euphorically towards Gandesa: "Oh we came to sunny

Spain to make the people smile again. And to drive the fascist bastards from the hill and from the plain…"

The train terminated at Dieppe and we walked to the docks where a ferry waited. It was exactly a year since I had crossed the Channel to take up arms against the fascists. I left for Spain on a memorable, clear night with Jack Jones and Kevin Rebecchi. On this return trip I stood on deck with Frank West, in weak April sunshine, eager for the sight of dear old England. It was a perfect crossing and we soon disembarked at Newhaven. Waiting for us were members of the International Brigade Association[53] and some gentlemen from Scotland Yard, who wished to talk to us about our activities in Spain.

But we were not detained for long. Back in London, we were taken to a co-operative warehouse and fitted with a new set of clothes. News of our release had only just filtered through to England, and there had been no time to alert the families. I concluded my active service with the International Brigade by catching a bus home to Battersea.

The fates had arranged a gathering of my family and close friends on that very night. I could hear laughter and music as I walked through the front door of our terraced house to surprise my father, my mother, my sister and brother. From a corner of our parlour I heard an old friend shout:

"Where the bloody hell have you been?"

Endnotes

1. George's 'Black Hole of Calcutta' analogy refers to an incident from early British colonial history. In 1756 the Nawab of Bengal attacked and occupied Calcutta, then a possession of the East India Company. Nearly 150 people were said to have been imprisoned overnight in a small, airless dungeon. In the morning the majority were found dead from suffocation. The story was evidently embellished, and possibly contrived, in order to demonise the native population.

2. The *Guardia Civil* is a paramilitary rural police force whose officers tended to side with the Nationalists during the Civil War and acted as enthusiastic agents of the Franco repression.

3. More than twenty-seven countries, including Germany and Italy, signed the Non-Intervention Agreement. It was hoped that by denying arms and ammunition to both sides, the conflict would fizzle out.

4. Aneurin Bevan was a left-wing Labour MP who campaigned for the Spanish Republic at a time when official Labour Party policy was to endorse non-intervention. As Minister of Health in Attlee's post-war Labour government, he oversaw the creation of the National Health Service.

5. The 1870 Foreign Enlistment Act was passed at the outbreak of the Franco-Prussian War and made it an

offence for a British subject to enlist in or recruit for the forces of a foreign power.

6. George, like most working-class volunteers, did not possess a passport. At the time the railways advertised weekend trips to Paris, leaving Victoria Station on Friday nights, for which passports were not required.

7. Jack Jones was one of four Labour Party councillors to serve in the British Battalion. Appointed Political Commissar of No. 1 (the Major Attlee) Company, he was wounded at the Battle of the Ebro and repatriated to Britain. His experiences in Spain are recounted in the autobiography *Union Man*. Celebrating his ninetieth birthday in February 2003, he is still active in the T & G Union's retired members' association.

8. Kevin Rebecchi grew up in a Catholic family in the Melbourne suburb of Brunswick. Aged twenty-one when he arrived in Spain, Rebecchi was wounded in the attacks on Hill 481 and died from Typhus in hospital in the northern Catalonian town of Vic in January 1939.

9. James McNeill was born in Sydney in 1900. A sheet metal worker and member of the Communist Party of Australia, McNeill was wounded in the 'last action' in September 1938. Rebecchi and McNeill were among seventy Australians who served in Spain on the side of the Republic. Their story is told in Amirah Inglis's *Australians in Spain*.

10. Arthur Jamieson was, as George suggests, from Manchester. Wounded at the Ebro, he spent time in hospital at Figueras and left Spain for Perpignan in October 1938.

11. James Alexander Bayne came from Garden City, Long Island, New York. Aged twenty-four when he arrived in Spain, Bayne survived the war and returned to the USA in December 1938.

12. Constantine 'Gus' Mikadis was from McKeesport, Pennsylvania. Wounded in the Ebro battles, he returned to the USA aged twenty-three and died after an operation to remove a bullet from his neck.

13. The commissar system in the International Brigades was inherited from the Russian Red Army. Political Commissars operated at brigade, battalion and company level. Their principal responsibility was to look after and monitor the welfare, morale and discipline of the volunteers.

14. Harold Horne was born in Willesden, north London in 1910. A fitter by trade and a graduate of the Lenin School in Moscow, Horne arrived in Spain in August 1937. He was badly wounded during the Aragon retreats in March 1938 and again during the Ebro fighting. He was repatriated with the British Battalion in December 1938.

15. Frank Proctor came from Liverpool and was aged about nineteen when he arrived in Spain in May 1937. Assigned to a British Anti-Tank Battery, he was later

transferred to the British Battalion. Seriously wounded in the battles in the Sierra Pandols in August 1938, he died in hospital.

16. *Chabola* is a Spanish word for a hut or lean-to, hence the unofficial name for the valley where the Battalion sheltered and trained before the Ebro Offensive.

17. Bert Sines was born in Battersea, south London. A veteran of the First World War, Sines was a shop assistant, a member of the Communist Party and the TGWU. He arrived in Spain in December 1936 and was wounded at the Battle of Jarama in February 1937. He was also wounded at the Ebro and was repatriated to England in October 1938.

18. David Guest was the son of Labour MP Dr. Leslie Haden Guest. He was born in London in 1911 and educated at Oundle School and Cambridge and Göttingen universities. A member of the Young Communist League he served on Battersea Council alongside George's father. Guest left a teaching position at University College Southampton to volunteer for Spain. He was killed in the attacks on Hill 481. In 1939 his mother, the writer Carmel Haden Guest, edited a touching memoir *David Guest. A Scientist Fights for Freedom.*

19. Nearly three thousand Americans volunteered to fight for the Spanish Republic. By mid 1937 two battalions had been formed, the Abraham Lincoln and the George Washington. After the bloodbath at the Battle of Brunete, Washington survivors were absorbed into

the Lincoln Battalion. A moving account can be found in Peter Carroll's *The Odyssey of the Abraham Lincoln Brigade* (sic).

20. Harry Shepard Jr. came from Muskogee, Oklahoma. A newspaper reporter, he arrived in Spain in March 1938 aged twenty-four. He was wounded in action during the Ebro Offensive and returned to the USA in December 1938.

21. *Mexicanskis* were Mosin-Nagant rifles made in the USA by Remington for the Russian Tsarist army. Quantities were sold by the Soviet Union to Mexico and subsequently shipped back across the Atlantic to Republican Spain.

22. More than fifteen hundred Canadians fought for the Spanish Republic. In the early months of the conflict, volunteers were scattered throughout the various International Brigades. As numbers increased, a battalion was created and named in honour of William Lyon MacKenzie and Louis-Joseph Papineau, leaders of the failed 1837 rebellion against British rule in Canada. Together with the British and the Americans, the MacKenzie-Papineau Battalion formed the core of the 15th Brigade. Mark Zuehlke's *The Gallant Cause* is a readable and affectionate study of Canadians in Spain.

23. Sam Wild was born in Ardwick, Manchester in 1908. From a Catholic background, the innately rebellious Wild joined the Royal Navy, which he deserted when

his ship docked at Simonstown in South Africa. A boilermaker and member of the Labour Party, he volunteered for Spain in December 1936. He was wounded at the battles of Jarama and Brunete and commanded No. 3 Company at Teruel. Wild became Battalion Commander in February 1938, a position he held until the volunteers were repatriated the following December. While commanding the Battalion, he was promoted to major and awarded the Spanish Republic's highest military honour.

24. Robert Hunt Cooney came from a Catholic family in Aberdeen. A shop assistant and member of the Communist Party, he studied at the Lenin School in Moscow. Aged thirty when he arrived in Spain, the popular, boyish-looking Cooney was appointed Battalion Political Commissar. His unpublished memoir *Proud Journey* can be found in the International Brigade Archive at Marx House in London.

25. Arding & Hobbs is a traditional department store still trading at Clapham Junction just down the hill from George's old home in Battersea.

26. Juan Modesto was a former Spanish Foreign Legion corporal who rose rapidly to command the Republican forces during the Ebro Offensive.

27. 'Moors' is a generic term for the Arab and Berber mercenary soldiers from Spanish Morocco who served in the Nationalist 'Army of Africa'.

28. The 13th 'Dombrowski' Brigade initially consisted of Polish, Balkan, French and Franco-Belgian battalions. By the time of the Ebro Offensive it was essentially Slavic in composition.

29. The British Battalion in the field consisted of three rifle companies and one machine gun company. The structure of the British Battalion and the organisation of the International Brigades are outlined in the Osprey publication *International Brigades in Spain 1936-1939* by Ken Bradley and Mike Chappell.

The first history of the British Battalion, *Britons in Spain* by the Daily Worker correspondent Bill Rust, was published in 1939. After a historiographical gap of forty years, Judith Cook's *Apprentices of Freedom* made extensive use of taped interviews with British veterans from the Imperial War Museum's sound archive. In 1982 Bill Alexander, a former Battalion Commander, brought out *British Volunteers for Liberty*, a comprehensive, if somewhat doctrinaire account.

More recently the American historian James T. Hopkins's *Into the Heart of the Fire* placed the British contingent in a broad political, social and cultural framework. In 2002 Richard Baxell completed a PhD thesis at the LSE entitled *The British Battalion of the International Brigades in the Spanish Civil War 1936-1939*. This outstanding work sets the 21st century standard and is required reading for anyone interested in the subject.

30. John Dunlop was born in Winnipeg, Canada, to Scottish parents in 1915 and grew up in Edinburgh. From a middle-class background, he was educated at a private school and trained to be an accountant. A member of the Communist Party, he arrived in Spain in May 1937 and joined the British Anti-Tank Battery. He served at the Jarama Front and was wounded at Brunete. Assigned to the machine gun company he fought at Teruel and Belchite and was transferred to George's rifle company, before the Ebro Offensive. Dunlop returned to Britain with the Battalion in December 1938. Along with Steve Fullarton and James Maley, he is one of only three surviving Scottish veterans in February 2003.

31. Enrique Lister was a rough, single-minded, Moscow-trained general who commanded an army corps at the Battle of the Ebro.

32. Lawrence Pryme was a Londoner and member of the Communist Party. Wounded on Hill 481 on 27 July 1938, he died in hospital in Barcelona a month later.

33. Lewis Clive was born in London in 1910. He was said to be a direct descendant of Clive of India and came from a landed family in Herefordshire. A godson of Conservative politician Neville Chamberlain, he was educated at Eton and Oxford where he gained a rowing blue. He subsequently won a gold medal rowing for Britain in the 1932 Los Angeles Olympics. Narrowly avoiding a career in banking, Clive became a socialist and wrote a book on military theory called *People's Army*.

Like Jack Jones, he was a Labour Party councillor when he volunteered to fight in Spain. Clive's rowing days at Oxford, his early adult life in London and decision to join the International Brigade are chronicled in *Muck, Silk and Socialism*, the recent, posthumous autobiography of his best friend, the New Zealand-born QC and former Labour MP, John Platts-Mills.

34. Leslie John Brickell was a miner from Tredegar in south Wales. Wounded at the Ebro, he returned from hospital to the Battalion and was captured near Corbera on 23 September 1938. Welsh miners made up one of the largest contingents in the British Battalion, as demonstrated in Hywel Francis's *Miners Against Fascism. Wales and the Spanish Civil War.* In February 2003 just three known Welsh veterans survive: Alun Williams from the Rhondda, Edwin Greening from Aberdare and Bob Peters, a Penarth man who had emigrated to Canada but returned to Europe to join the International Brigade.

35. Samuel H. White is possibly the 'Snowy' referred to by George. A labourer from Edinburgh, he was captured at Corbera during the 'last action' and released in April 1939.

36. George's jovial friend may have been one of three Swedish volunteers: Karl Edvin Nilsson from Malmo, Karl Erik Nilsson from Karlstad or Karl Ingemar Nilsson from Pitea. The first two returned to Sweden, the third is listed as 'missing'.

37. John Leith Walker was born in Fife, Scotland, in 1898. A member of the Labour Party, he worked as a labourer in London. Arriving in Spain in August 1937, Walker was assigned to the *Intendencia*, or Battalion stores, as Quartermaster.

38. Ernest Sim was originally from Aberdeen. Working in London as a labourer he volunteered for Spain in October 1937 at the age of twenty-three. He was killed in action on 8 August 1938.

39. The term 'British' Battalion was something of a misnomer. From its inception the Battalion counted men from Ireland, North America, Australia, New Zealand, South Africa, Cyprus and elsewhere. Spaniards had always been present, but by the time of the Ebro Offensive - and as a result of attrition in Spain and a dwindling supply of volunteers from Britain - the Battalion was a substantially Spanish military formation.

40. With the failure if the Ebro Offensive, the Republic faced certain defeat. As part of a formula for a negoti-ated peace, it proposed the withdrawal of all foreign volunteers from Spain.

41. Cyril Frank West was born in 1907 in London. A member of the Communist Party, he lived in Shepherd's Bush and worked as a caterer. He arrived in Spain in September 1937 and became Political Commissar of No. 2 Company.

42. Thomas McGuire was born in Greenock, Scotland. He lived in London and worked as a labourer. A section leader in No. 4 Company he was captured with George and released in February 1939. In the Second World War he served in the Parachute Regiment and was killed in North Africa in 1943.

43. Technically not fascists, the *Requetés* were extremist Carlist militiamen from rural Navarre who advocated the creation of a theocratic Spanish state to be ruled by warrior priests.

44. James Pollock came from Glasgow but was working as a clerk in Bury, Lancashire at the time of the rebellion. He arrived in Spain in March 1938 and was captured with George. Pollock served in the British Army in the Second World War and was killed in action.

45. In *British Volunteers for Liberty*, Bill Alexander (Battalion Commander before Sam Wild) writes that 'Battalion strength on the night of 22 September was 377, of whom 106 were British. When it withdrew on the night of the 24th it was 173 strong of whom 58 were British. Two hundred men were killed, missing or taken prisoner'.

From the British and Irish volunteers captured on the same day as George, one especially poignant personal story emerges. Nineteen-year-old James Haughey was a practising Catholic from Lurgan, Co. Armagh, Northern Ireland. Anticipating execution, he asked his Nationalist captors for a priest. That a foreign godless red should ask to confess his sins was interpreted as mockery, if not blasphemy, and Haughey was severely beaten for his impertinent request.

After release from prison, anecdotal evidence suggests young Haughey was reluctant to return to Northern Ireland. Apparently he was worried that news of his service with the International Brigade would bring shame to his equally devout family. He swapped identity papers with John Kambides, a Greek Canadian volunteer who wished to stay in Europe, and was 'repatriated' to Canada.

In the Second World War Haughey enlisted, under his own name, in the Royal Canadian Airforce. A warrant officer, serving as a wireless operator and air gunner, he was killed in a flying accident in Devon in 1943. He is buried in a Catholic cemetery at home in Lurgan.

46. Maurice Levitas was born to a Jewish family in Dublin in 1917. Moving to London, he worked as a plumber's mate. A member of the Communist Party, he arrived in Spain in January 1938 and was captured at Calaceite the following March.

47. Who indeed was Tinker Fry? There are two possible candidates for this curious exchange: Frank Tinker was an American mercenary fighter pilot who flew for the Spanish Republic. George may have misheard the question, 'Who was Tinker, Frank? Alternatively it may have been a reference to Harold Fry, a prominent Scottish volunteer who was captured by the Nationalists and later released. Breaking the

conditions of his parole, he returned to Spain and was killed in action. It may simply be the case that George's interrogators were talking nonsense, a condition not unassociated with fascism.

48. David Hyman Wallach was born in Poland in 1914. A shipping clerk from Brooklyn, New York, he was a member of the Young Communist League. Arriving in Spain in January 1938, Wallach was captured during the retreats in April 1938. In the Second World War he served with American forces in North Africa, Sicily and Italy.

49. David Fleming Kennedy was born in Ballycastle, Co. Antrim, Northern Ireland in 1915. He moved to Greenock, Scotland, where he worked as a painter. Arriving in Spain in February 1938, he was captured a month later at Calaceite. Numerous Irishmen served with the British, American and Canadian contingents in Spain. In February 2003 only three survive: Eugene Downing, Bob Doyle and Michael O'Riordan.

50. Mykola 'Nick' Elendiuk may well have been a cowboy, but he began life in Lithuania in 1911 and emigrated to Canada. He left for Spain from Winnipeg in Canada's mid-west.

51. Charles T. Matthews was born in London in 1919. A clerk and member of the Young Communist League, he arrived in Spain in March 1938. He was captured near Corbera on the same day as George. Just over thirty British and Irish veterans survive; of the

volunteers who appear in George's narrative, only Matthews, Jones and Dunlop are alive in February 2003.

52. Every repatriated volunteer received a bill from the Foreign Office for £2-4-11^d. The majority, on a point of principle, refused to pay.

53. The International Brigade Association was formed in March 1939 to continue the 'anti-fascist struggle' and to look after the interests of the returned volunteers. In 2002 the IBA merged with the Friends of the International Brigade to form the International Brigade Memorial Trust, an organisation with charitable status.

Index

K

Kennedy, David 184

L

Levitas, Maurice 183
Lister, Enrique 89, 99, 179

M

MacKenzie-Papineau Battalion 59, 112, 176
Marçà 20,53,59
Matthews, Charles T 184
McGuire, Thomas 121, 181
McNeill, Jim 173
Mexicanski rifle 176
Mikadis 45, 174
Modesto, Juan 70, 177
Montblanc 49, 50, 52, 54, 134
Moors 67, 177

N

Nilsson, Karl 109, 180
Non-Intervention Agreement 172

P

Paris 38,39
Pollock, James 182
Proctor, Frank 174
Pryme, Lawrence 76, 79, 170, 179
Pyrenees 18,41,42,45,

R

Rebecchi, Kevin 38, 53, 171, 173
Requetés 119,182

S

San Pedro de Cardeña 38, 39, 134, 173
San Sebastián 163,164,165,169,170
Shepard, Harry 176
Sierra Pandols 20,89,91,93,170,175
Sim, Ernest 170

T

Tivissa 105,107,108,111,170,

W

Walker, 'Hookey' 112
Wallach, Hyman 184
West, Frank 117, 118, 165, 171, 181
White, Samuel 180
Wild, Sam 59, 63, 176, 182

Z

Zaragoza 129, 131, 162

For further information about Zymurgy Publishing and other independent publishers please access the following web site http://www.ipg.uk.com. All Zymurgy titles may be ordered from all good book shops.

Natural North
by Allan Potts
Foreword by the Duke of Northumberland

A photographic celebration of flora and fauna in the North of England. Supporting text provides background information. Sections cover; high fells, upland, woodland, agricultural, coastal and urban areas.
ISBN 1 903506 00X hb 160pp £16.99

Bent Not Broken
by Lauren Roche

Lauren Roche's autobiography; an abused child, stowaway, stripper, prostitute, drug abuser. She turned her life around to become a doctor. An international best seller. Lauren has been interviewed by Lorraine Kelly, Esther Rantzen, Johnny Walker, Simon Mayo and others.
ISBN 1 903506 026 pb 272pp £6.99

A Lang Way To The Pawnshop
by Thomas Callaghan
Introduction by Sid Chaplin

An autobiographical account of growing up in 1930s urban Britain; a family of ten, two bedrooms, no wage earner. An amusing insight into a period of history still in living memory.
ISBN 1 903506 018 pb 144pp £6.99

The Krays: The Geordie Connection
by Steve Wraith and Stuart Wheatman
Foreword by Dave Courtney

After seeing the Krays' at a funeral on the news (aged ten) Steve writes letters, meets the brothers and eventually becomes one of 'the chaps'. The book is about the Krays' final years and how they ran things on the outside.
ISBN 1 903506 042 pb 240pp £6.99

The River Tyne From Sea to Source
by Ron Thornton
Foreword by Robson Green

A collection of nearly eighty water colours and hundreds of pencil drawings following the River Tyne from outside the harbour to the source of the North and South Tyne rivers. Supporting text provides a wealth of information on the history surrounding the Tyne.
ISBN 1 903506 034 hb 160pp £16.99

Life On The Line
by Lauren Roche

Following on from Bent Not Broken the book covers Lauren's life once she becomes a doctor. Bankruptcy, depression, a suicide attempt - and the shock revelation that her son was a sex offender. What can a mother do when she suspects that one of her children is being abused? What happens when you discover that the abused child has become an abuser?
ISBN 1 903506 050 pb 192pp £6.99